MW01097324

VICTORINOX
SWISS ARMY
KNIVES

A COLLECTOR'S COMPANION

DEREK JACKSON
updated by PATRICK HOOK

CHARTWELL BOOKS

Acknowledgments

My thanks to Victorinox—particularly Urs Wyss—for supplying background material, allowing me to dig through their company archives, and for permission to use company and personal photographs, as well as illustrations from their centenary book *The Knife and its History*.

Brimming with creative inspiration, how-to projects, and useful information to enrich your everyday life, Quarto Knows is a favorite destination for those pursuing their interests and passions. Visit our site and dig deeper with our books into your area of interest: Quarto Creates, Quarto Cooks, Quarto Homes, Quarto Lives, Quarto Drives, Quarto Explores, Quarto Gifts, or Quarto Kids.

This edition published in 2018 by
Chartwell Books
an imprint of Book Sales
a division of Quarto Publishing Group USA Inc.
142 West 36th Street, 4th Floor
New York, New York 10018
USA
T (212) 779-4972 F (212) 779-6058
www.QuartoKnows.com

ISBN: 978-0-7858-3634-6

Printed and bound in China

10 9 8 7 6 5 4 3 2 1

From a basic design by Frank Ainscough
Redesigned by EF Designs

Contents

INTRODUCTION

Switzerland is not a country that many people associate with war today; however, its inhabitants have a long history of involvement with military matters, and they are among the most fiercely defensive anywhere. Although it is not a major steel-producing country, the Swiss Army Knife, originally produced by a Swiss master cutler for the Swiss armed forces, is now recognized throughout the world. Like the Rolls-Royce or the Zippo lighter, it has become part of the mythology of the 20th century and represents a standard of quality and versatility which has carried through into the 21st century.

The basic design of the knife has changed little since Karl Elsener patented the first "Swiss Officer's Knife" in 1897, but the context within which the knives are now used would have astonished him. Elsener's knives have been used at the top of Mount Everest and on coral reefs; astronauts carry them in the Space Shuttle; they have saved lives on the ocean, in the air, and in the desert.

When Karl Elsener founded the company we know today as Victorinox, he was working against the odds. His home district of Schwyz, in German-speaking Switzerland was a rural area, with very little industry and no tradition of knife-making. The Swiss armed forces presented the only opportunity for a substantial order, but their soldier's knives were

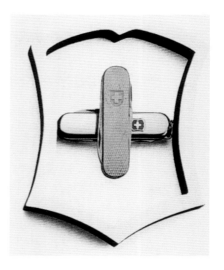

ABOVE: Victorinox advertising has always been stylish — here is a play on the Swiss emblem that appears on every Victorinox knife.
RIGHT: 23,000 electrical Swiss Army Knife displays are placed in shops and shop windows all over the world.

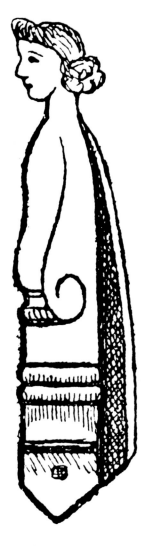

The idea for a hinged knife blade that folds into its own handle has been around for many years. This is an image of a pocket knife unearthed in Rome.

supplied by the large German factories at a price which no small workshop could match. Elsener persevered and, with imagination, commitment and an obsession for quality, he built a company which today supplies the German army with knives and sells more than 25% of its output to America, the world's largest producer of pocket knives.

Although the name "Swiss Army Knife" is almost a generic term for the multi-bladed pocket knife, these knives have been around for a very long time. The Romans produced folding knives and there are many examples in museums of multi-bladed knives from every era since then. A blade of some kind is used by almost every craftsman in the world and the need to carry a favorite tool safely at all times has led to some ingenious designs. US knife makers have been producing superb folding knives since the start of the American steel industry and, before the Second World War, the Swiss knives were known only to Swiss nationals and to a very few connoisseurs in other parts of Europe. At the end of the war Victorinox started selling their "Officer's Knives" through the American military's PX stores, the servicemen recognized their

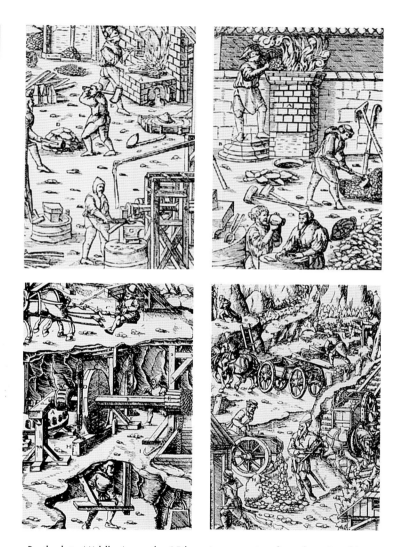

By the late Middle Ages—the 15th century—most surface deposits of iron had been exhausted and iron ore had to be mined. The growing need for metal meant that there were many centers of production and much experimentation in techniques—to help with deep extraction; the use of water power to help with hammering and blowing air onto the fires (use of water wheels means larger belows and greater temperatures); and the use of plateways and, later, railroads.

lakeside settlements in France and Switzerland, from Scandinavia and from the Gold Coast. Some of the hafts are worked with decorative patterns. Bronze Age knives with tangs (or tongues) protruding into the handle are the most common, typical examples came from sites around Lakes Neuchâtel and Geneva in Switzerland. In many cases the backs and surfaces of the blades are richly decorated. The ferrule type seems to have been most popular in these areas. The ferrules are long and conical, set in line with the blade, with one or two holes bored through them for receiving pins or rivets for attaching the handle.

The Iron Age

The production of iron and steel had an extraordinary impact on the development of human civilisation. With the development of this strong, malleable material came a massive surge in man's ability to manipulate his environment, through agriculture, the use of more sophisticated weapons and the development of more intricate and sophisticated tools for all sorts of manufacturing processes.

Yet iron first emerged as a precious metal, used only for decorative brooches, buckles, rings and bracelets. Finds in Mesopotamian burial sites

at Warka and Mongheir (now in Iraq) have provided us with proof that iron was used for making small decorative objects as far back as 25 to 30 centuries BCE and in Egypt the use of iron for small objects also appears to date back to 3000 BCE. Egyptian pyramid drawings show us the processes involved in melting and casting the ore.

As with many inventions, the skills of iron extraction and working appear to have developed in areas as far apart as China and Europe within a relatively short timescale. We cannot know for sure whether the skills were passed from East to West, or simply reflected man's universal curiosity and urge for improvement. Legends from the classical era tell us that the first skills in metal working, originally deemed holy, came through the islands from Asia Minor to Greece.

In Greek religion, Hephaestus, the god of fire, was portrayed as a blacksmith and was patron of the smith's craft. His Roman counterpart was Vulcan, the divine blacksmith, forging thunderbolts for Jove. In both the Norse and Celtic religions the art of metalworking is also venerated. In Norse mythology, Mimir, the smith who taught the hero Siegfried his craft, was regarded as the wisest of the gods. The Celtic god Goibniu not only forged weapons for his fellow gods, but had the power of healing.

Classical writers give the cradle of metalworking as the area around the Black Sea, known as the land of the Chalybes; their name was synonymous with iron and Herodotus describes them as 'people who mined the earth and wrought iron'.

BELOW: John Russell Manufacturing Company, Turners Falls, MA, in 1884. The company was founded in 1834. The grinding room at John Russell's in about 1880, when about 70 men worked in it.

OPPOSITE: Monasteries, as in so many other disciplines, were repositories of knowledge. This is an image of the ironmasters of Chartreux.

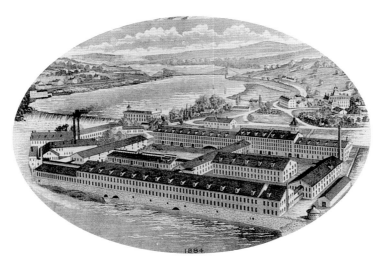

From Homer's writings come proof that steel was produced in Greece as early as 900 BCE. In his Odyssey he writes "the smith dips a large battle-axe or chopper into cold water to harden it amid a great hissing (since iron needs hardness)..." and many illustrations of the smith's art survive in Roman art.

In the early Chinese and Japanese civilisations weapons were certainly being made from iron as early as 2,500 BCE. Although there are records that the Celts produced iron implements from about 1,000 BCE it appears that most of the central European tribes would buy their steel from the East.

By 600 BCE, we know that Etruscans were working iron ore mines on the island of Elba, and iron knives and weapons existed in France, Switzerland and Germany at the same time. The Romans employed iron for household and agricultural implements and Pliny attributes the discovery of hardened steel to the Spanish, who have had a very ancient reputation for their highly finished, flexible blades.

During the period from 600 BCE in Europe iron tools and weapons gradually replaced those made from bronze. Apart from weapons for war and hunting, our forebears used knives of every shape and size in

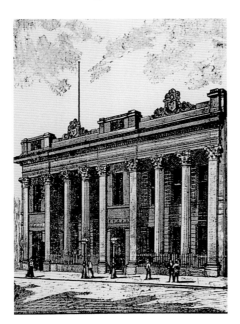

The Hall of the Company of Cutlers, a wonderful 19th century building in Sheffield, a city known for cutlery as early as Chaucer's time. (A Sheffield knife is mentioned in the *Canterbury Tales* in the *Reeves Tale*.) Forging blades for table knives in Sheffield. By 1864, Sheffield provided employment for over 12,000 workers involved in the cutlery industry.

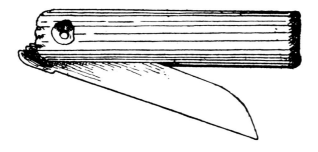

19th century Chinese penknife.

the home, workshop, and fields, from crudely formed blades to scissors with springs. Single purpose knives were produced to suit the specialized tasks of various craftsmen including farriers, shoemakers, and farmers. Hunting knives developed an overall size, proportion, and balance that has changed little over the centuries. The problem of devising the safest and most convenient way of carrying knives has been solved in many ways, with sheaths made from every conceivable material over the centuries, including animal horns, various woods, mother-of-pearl, bone, leather, metals, plastics and porcelain. Knives which folded into their own handle were an early development, though the introduction of springs to keep the blade in place came later—the first known folding knife is a Roman model from the 1st century AD, so Victorinox have taken their inspiration from the very earliest sources.

Louis XV (1715–1774) bayonet knife with pin. A pin secured the two-part haft of the knife, which held the blade in the closed position. When the pin was removed, the blade swivelled into an open position and was secured there by the same pin.

Similar idea, but this Louis XV knife has a combination lock at the end of the haft.

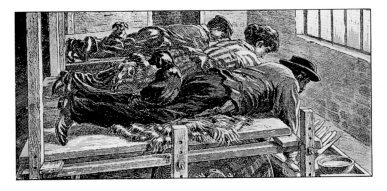

The knife grinder's art could be backbreaking. Here grinders, lying flat out on their bed planks, control a grip into which the blades were inserted for grinding. Dogs lie on their legs to warm them up and prevent rheumatism.

The Production Of Iron And Steel

Iron is obtained from iron ore through smelting, the dissolving of iron out of the non-ferrous elements of the ore and the chemical bindings. The oldest form of iron smelting was done in a Renn or bloomery furnace. The simplest type is a pit filled with iron ore and charcoal. From earliest times people have found ways to increase the draught to the fire, raising the temperature and increasing the efficiency of the smelting. In illustrations from Egyptian tombs smiths used foot pumps as bellows.

Knives from St Etienne, France, 18th century.

Mechanised forging of blades at J. A. Henckels,
Solingen, Germany. From the 15th to the 19th
century, Solingen was the largest producer of
knives and cutlery in Germany. Grinding shops at J. A. Henckels,
Solingen—a company still
working today. The
blockade of Europe in
Napoleon's time was
a boon to German
manufacturers, freed from
competition with Sheffield
cutlery.

American folding knives from
the Southington Cutlery Co,
Southington, Connecticut.

Once bricked-up shaft kilns were developed, oxygen was forced into the kiln through bellows, first powered by hand and later by water. In 13th century Europe larger shaft kilns were built, forming so-called lump furnaces. They were followed in the 16th century by flux furnaces which produced about 3,300lb of pig iron daily with a charcoal consumption of 8,250lb. Around 880lb of dry wood was needed to make 220lb of charcoal, so that 2.5 acres of woodland were destroyed to produce just 10 tons of iron. The pig iron produced in this way is still impure, containing 3-5% carbon and other elements. Only by burning off the unwanted side elements, especially sulphur and phosphorus, at temperatures of up to 3,632°F, reducing the carbon content to 0.3-1%, is steel fit for hardening obtained. Steel blades were heated to about 1,472°F and quickly cooled in water or oil to temper them.

Furnaces were refined and developed over the centuries, but a revolution in the production of steel occurred at the end of the nineteenth century with experiments in the use of electricity to power furnaces. The German-born British inventor Sir William Siemens first demonstrated the electric arc furnace in 1879 at the Paris Exposition by melting iron in crucibles. In this furnace, carbon electrodes produced an electric arc above the container of metal. The first commercial arc furnace in the United States was installed in 1906 with a capacity of four tons. Modern furnaces range in size from a few tons to 400 tons, with the arcs striking directly into the metal bath. The electric arc furnace is now used for

This is a 19th century Maniago knife; note the scissors and spring mechanism. Cutlery is still produced at Maniago, Venice, as it has been since Roman times.

the production of most steel throughout the world. Throughout the 19th century scientists in all the major iron producing countries were experimenting with the addition of alloys to give new properties to steel. In 1820, James Stodart and Michael Faraday, working in Britain, added gold and silver to steel in an attempt to improve its corrosion resistance. The mixtures could never have been commercially viable, but they led to the idea of adding chromium to steel and, eventually, to the development of stainless steel.

Work on the production of a corrosion-resistant steel suitable for use in armaments and machinery continued throughout the century and it is surprising that it was not until 1914 that a commercially viable material was developed. This was a composition of 0.4% carbon and 13% chromium, developed by Harry Brearly in Sheffield, England, then the most prolific producers of cutlery in the world. The Krupp works in Germany soon followed with a mixture of 18% chromium and 8% nickel. By 1920 the process of making a truly 'stainless' steel had been perfected and was in use throughout Europe and North America.

The early stainless steel was ideal for use in machinery, but was difficult to sharpen to a fine edge. A continuous process of refinement has taken place since the 1920s, and today's stainless steels have a high carbon content and produce extremely sharp blades.

Another 19th century Maniago pocket knife.

The Cutler's Craft

Knife making as a respected art form developed first in respect of weapons. From the Tai Ka period in Japan (around 560 BCE) blades of the very finest quality were produced and changed hands for fabulous amounts. Western legends feature swords such as Excalibur as prized possessions, often attributed with magical powers. However, in Europe it was not until the early Middle Ages (10th to 11th century) that cutlers making household knives and other implements for daily life began to be recognized as master craftsmen. Working conditions were primitive and each worker had to be able not only to make every single component, but also to forge his own tools.

The manufacture of knives universally includes five basic processes. First the metal is forged; after heating, a bar of metal is put between forging bars and hammered to a rough shape—now this is done using mechanical hammers from bars of steel—and the excess is trimmed to shape. After forging, the blades are hardened by heating and cooling in a liquid or between cooled metal plates. The blades are then tempered by reheating to the correct temperature to give them flexibility and toughness. The next process is grinding, using an abrasive substance to sharpen and shape the blade. The blade has to be kept cool during grinding to maintain its temper.

The grinding room at John Russell's in about 1880, when about 70 men worked in it.

22

The cutler as seen by Larmessin.

Examples of knives from the 16th to 18th centuries.

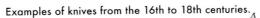

After grinding, the surface of the blade is given a finer finish in successive operations known as glazing and buffing, sometimes followed by mirror polishing, or "satin" finishing. The hafts are also ground, glazed and polished and finally fitted to the handle material.

Cutlery production became established in areas where there was plentiful timber for furnaces and charcoal in addition to soft water for tempering steel. Medieval grindstones were sometimes hand operated, but animal or water power was increasingly used to revolve treadmills or wheels. From about 1200 onwards major centers of cutlery manufacture grew up in Sheffield in England, in Paris, France and in Solingen, Germany. During the Renaissance Italian cutlers, mainly working in Milan and Venice, were thought of as the best in Europe and under the Bourbons all domestic knives for princes of royal blood were made in Italy. There are no records of cutlery manufacture in Switzerland before the 17th century, when a Cutler's Guild grew up in Aarau. Individual craftsmen and their apprentices have been making special purpose knives in Switzerland since then, but supplies for the armed forces came from the larger German workshops and factories right up until Karl Elsener's first Swiss Army Soldier's Knife was manufactured in 1891.

Cutlery making in Indochina. Note the lack of a round turning grindstone. The East did not invent these and ground blades by rubbing them on lumps of sandstone. The cutler as seen by Larmessin.

The Trusty Pocket Knife

As many owners of modern day Swiss Army Knives will testify, the knife is a very personal object. In all the metal producing cultures of history 'pocket' knives have existed, even before the invention of sewn-on pockets. From Roman times through to the present day individual craftsmen have fashioned exquisite folding knives, some with multiple blades, which have become an essential part of the equipment for most working people in addition to the more specialist tools of their trade. Intricate catches and locks were designed to hold the knife closed and to prevent it from closing during use until 1742, when Benjamin Huntsman, a clockmaker from Sheffield in England, developed a reliable steel spring mechanism which became the pattern for today's more sophisticated folding knives.

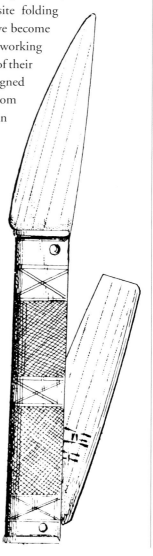

The blades and attachments to pocket knives are limited only by the size and weight of the finished knife, and by the imagination of the cutler. During the Middle Ages in Europe a personal knife was essential for anyone travelling away from home, as cutlery was not provided. A simple blade for slicing off chunks of food was enough, but collectors today have gathered many examples from Renaissance times to the present day of folding cutlery sets with knife, fork and even spoons fitting neatly into an ornate handle.

Folding knife from Indochina. Iron ore came from North Kampuchea, and the artists of Hanoi were renowned for their clever techniques, inlaying rare woods with mother-of-pearl.

Chapter 2

The Swiss Army

Switzerland is a country grown out of compromise and mutual interest. It is one of the very few truly multilingual countries which have managed to maintain a stable system of government while respecting the differences between its three major groups of citizens in the German, French, and Italian-speaking sectors. We think of the Swiss as peaceful people with no great military pretensions, but the stability of the Swiss Confederation has been won at great cost and defended with legendary military prowess. The mountains of Switzerland in Roman times were regarded as strategically important territory because the passes gave access to the Germanic tribes of the north who controlled vital resources for the economy of Rome. Switzerland at that time was part of Gaul and formed the interface between the civilized south and the barbarian hordes of the north.

Right up until the 14th century, the area we now think of as Switzerland formed the battleground for competing European powers. The people of the region, struggling to survive the harsh climate and

lack of natural resources, were ruled first by one distant power, then another, without any significant change in their condition. Their response was to build societies based on mutual aid and loyalty to the home region and family. The land could not support an ever-growing population, but the skills needed to thrive in the mountains were in demand elsewhere.

Swiss mercenaries became famous throughout Europe, giving the winning edge to whichever monarch was willing to pay their price. The early companies of Swiss, German, and Italian mercenaries were not the most loyal of soldiers. They were not concerned with the rights and wrongs of the territorial disputes for which they fought, and were apt to mutiny and would change sides if payment was not forthcoming. However, they were independent and self-sufficient, and could be relied on to be ruthless in battle when paid the right price.

The mercenaries of the mountain regions also had a profound effect on the development of modern warfare tactics. The land in the mountains of central Europe was too poor to support an armored elite and totally unsuited to mounted combat in heavy armor. When the crossbow appeared as a serious military weapon around the middle of the 9th century it gave the infantry a position of tactical dominance in mountain and skirmish warfare.

Crossbows were capable of killing the most powerful of mounted warriors, yet they were far cheaper than war-horses and armor and required far less skill and training than the Turkish or Mongol bow or the English longbow. The crossbow challenged the mounted elite's dominance in war, a point that Europe's rulers did not miss. In 1139 the second Lateran Council banned the crossbow as a weapon "hateful to God and unfit for Christians" and Emperor Conrad III of Germany forbade its use in his realms. Unfortunately for them, the crossbow proved too useful in the Crusades to be outlawed forever and underwent a continuous process of technical development that ended only in the 16th century, with its replacement by the harquebus and musket. The crossbow remains a strong symbol of Swiss independence and resistance to military threats, as witnessed by the legends surrounding the ultimate Swiss hero, William Tell.

The Swiss took the infantry another step forward in defence of their own territory in 1315 at the Battle of Morgaten. Faced with the armored knights of the Habsburg Invaders, they used 18-foot pikes, or spears with small, piercing heads. No longer outreached by the knight's lance, and displaying far greater cohesion than any knightly army, the peasant soldiers of Schwyz killed more than 1,500 knights, drove others into Lake Aegeri and put the rest to flight. Their victory ensured the survival of the Swiss Confederation and, with the pike square tactical formation, provided the model for the modern infantry regiment. The prestigious Swiss Guard at the Vatican in Rome still carry pikes as part of their ceremonial uniform.

The development of the Swiss Confederation as we know it today was not a smooth progression. The three mountain cantons of Uri, Schwyz and Unterwalden first cooperated in a partnership of mutual defence and were later joined by other communities suffering the same economic hardships and threats from neighboring powers.

By the beginning of the 15th century, eight cantons were allied, encircled by the powerful dynasties of Habsburg, Milan, Savoy and Burgundy. Vulnerable to attack, the Swiss turned from defensive tactics to offensive thrusts to secure their territory. The last Austrian outpost south of the Rhine, Aargau, which separated Zurich from Lucerne and Bern, was captured in 1415 and threats from Savoy to the southwest were resolved when Valais became allied with the confederation.

During the 15th century there was a continuous shuffling of alliances and more regions joined the confederation, incorporating German, French and Italian speaking communities. By the time of the French Revolution there were 13 cantons in the Helvetic Association. Each had its own army, religious antagonisms still existed; the rural cantons were suspicious of the towns and the small cantons were jealous of the larger ones. There was no central government and the cantons were ill-equipped to deal with the violent forces set loose throughout Europe.

The French took control of the region and established the Helvetic Republic, which lasted from 1798 to 1803. A single constitution, drawn up in Paris with little consideration for the proud, independent traditions of the Swiss cantons, was imposed from afar. The occupiers treated Switzerland as a vassal state, and it became a battlefield for the French and their enemies. The result was internal disorder, amounting almost to anarchy by the year 1803. Napoleon intervened with the Mediation Act, which stabilized the country. The Swiss remained neutral during the rest of the Napoleonic Wars, despite suffering economic hardships as a result of continental blockades. In 1815, after Napoleon's fall, the Congress of Vienna established the perpetual neutrality of the confederation. The confederation then included 25 of the 26 cantons still established in Switzerland today.

Internal wrangling between the various linguistic and religious groups continued through the 19th century, but a stable political and economic community of common interest gradually evolved. A new constitution, modelled after that of the United States, was established in 1848 and modified in 1974. Sovereignty was divided between the cantons and the federal state. Representatives to a federal government were elected either by a majority of the country's population or by the canton, thereby providing a fair representation of the smaller cantons. A common foreign policy was finally possible and the federal government undertook the protection of the rights and liberties of all citizens and the promotion of the nation's welfare.

In accordance with confederation neutrality, the army serves solely to preserve the independence of the country, a duty of every citizen. Defence is therefore based on a system of universal conscription under which every Swiss male is liable for military duties between the ages of 20 and 42 years, or, for officers, 20 and 47 years. The training of young recruits is followed by eight annual three-week refresher courses and later by shorter supplementary courses. Swiss women may serve as volunteers. The Swiss soldier keeps his equipment, including arms and ammunition, at home and performs his obligatory gunnery duty each year in civilian clothes. The Swiss army has a reputation as one of the best equipped infantry forces in the world and, though it has not been put to the test for many years, potential invaders would do well to remember the ferocious historical reputation of Swiss mercenaries and infantrymen. Self-sufficiency and the ability to co-operate as a force of independent individuals are the distinguishing features of the Swiss forces. It is no wonder, then that Switzerland has developed the ultimate symbol of readiness, the Swiss Army Knife.

The Soldier's Knife

The nature of weaponry has changed radically during the past 100 years. Soldiers, sailors and airmen in the western world are equipped with weapons and survival kits of unbelievable sophistication. Yet, when American pilot Scott O'Grady found himself alone in a hostile environment and in danger of capture during the Bosnian conflict, he relied on his Swiss Army Knife to help him survive the ordeal.

Soldiers have always carried knives. The Roman centurion would always have a small blade to supplement his main weapon, and to use for all his personal chores. A small, personal knife has been essential to the soldier or sailor throughout history: for the repair of clothing, footwear, harness or rigging; for use in cooking and eating; for cleaning and maintaining his weapons; as part of a drastic first aid kit; and to trim his beard, nails and hair. A simple blade will fulfil most of these functions adequately. A range of implements fitting neatly into the same space taken up by one blade must have been the soldier's dream come true.

A number of factors in the technology of warfare came together at the end of the 19th century to produce the need for the Swiss Army Knife. Horses were still used extensively for transporting men and equipment and a leather harness does wear out and break. A sharp, strong punch is much more efficient than the point of a knife for making repairs to leather, and the soldier on the move could not always call on the services of a fully equipped craftsman when repairs were needed.

Food was first preserved in sealed tins in about 1810, but it was another 50 years before the tin opener was invented. During those 50 years the cans were made of solid iron with a coating of tin inside. Each carried a label saying "Cut round the top with a chisel and hammer." Tin cans were ideal for carrying military provisions, providing enough food for one meal at a time, which could be cooked by the individual or small group of soldiers without the need for butchers and cooks. However, most soldiers would rebel at the idea of having to carry around a heavy hammer and chisel simply in order to open their food. Once lighter tins, with custom-made openers, had been developed, it was logical that every soldier should carry his own tin opener.

In 1889, the army of the Swiss Federation introduced a new rifle to be issued to all soldiers. To disassemble the rifle for cleaning, a screwdriver was needed. At this time the Swiss soldier was carrying a single-bladed folding knife, but it could not be made to perform all the functions now required of it. With no major center for knife production in Switzerland at that time, the army turned to a German manufacturer in the steel-producing town of Solingen and asked them to supply a multi-purpose tool small enough to be carried by their soldiers at all times. The original Swiss Soldier's Knife was produced in Solingen, complete with blade, tin opener, punch and screwdriver.

In 1891, Karl Elsener of Schwyz won the army contract for his Association of Swiss Master Cutlers and the "Original Swiss Army Knife" was born.

Chapter 3

Karl Elsner and the First
Swiss Army Knife

Karl Elsener, the founder of Victorinox, was born on October 9, 1860 in Schwyz, one of the three cantons to sign the Oath of Eternal Alliance in 1291, creating the Swiss Confederation. He came from a relatively wealthy family within an area where employment opportunities were limited. Karl was the fourth child of Balthasar and Victoria Elsener-Ott, who owned and managed a hat and felt workshop in the village of Schwyz. Victoria seems to have been a woman of prodigious energy, raising 12 children while running from the family home the hat shop in which the knives were sold.

Karl's older brother Dominik went into the family business, training to take over from his father the management of the factory. This left Karl to find his own profession and he decided to train as a master cutler. His first step in learning his craft was to return to the town of Zug, where the Elsener family can be traced back through nine

1867 photograph of the family of Balthasar and Victoria Elsener-Ott with their four eldest sons.

Karl Elsener (1860–1918), founder of Victorinox.

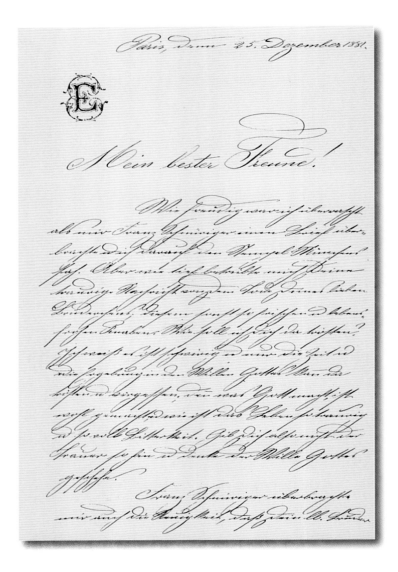

A letter dated Christmas day 1881 from Paris
to his friend Bernhard in Schilter shows that
even as an apprentice he was already
thinking of setting himself up as an
independent cutler in Schwyz.

ABOVE: Karl married a girl from Schwyz, Josepha (1861–1895), in September 1885. She died during the stillbirth of their ninth child.

RIGHT: This advertisement from 1884 announces the opening of Karl Elsener's workshop and his services as a maker of instruments for all professions requiring tools. He also offers a same-day repair and sharpening service.

Karl, Josepha, and children, Carl (7), Joseph (6), Anton (5), Alois (4), Marie (3), Hans (2), baby Balz in the pram behind, in about 1893.

generations to the 16th century. Relatives helped him to make a start on his career, but Switzerland at that time had no major cutlery industry and, if Karl wanted to become the best in his chosen profession, he would have to seek training from master craftsmen. He took up an apprenticeship in Paris, still a major center of the cutlery trade and renowned for products of superb workmanship. With this experience to recommend him, he then traveled to another major steel producing

The annual meeting of the Association of Swiss Master Cutlers was held on July 2, 1905. Karl Elsener is at the end on the right.

area and worked in the south German town of Tuttlingen, specialising in the making of razor knives and surgical instruments.

At that time Switzerland was among the poorest countries in Europe, with little industrial development and few opportunities for employment other than agriculture. However, Karl decided to return to his home town and try to build up a business of his own. He opened up a workshop in the former Koller mill on the Tobelbach in Ibach, Schwyz on January 1, 1884. The Tobelbach provided the power to drive a water wheel to which grinding and polishing machines were coupled.

Association of Swiss Master Cutlers

At this time the Swiss army bought knives for soldier's kits from Solingen in Germany, as there were no cutlers in Switzerland with the resources to fulfil such a large order to the required standard. In 1890 Elsener took the initiative of organizing the Association of Swiss Master Cutlers with the object of co-operation between all members to develop what no single cutler could then achieve; a pocket knife made for the Swiss army in Switzerland.

Some 25 fellow cutlers participated and the first delivery was made in 1891. The original Soldier's Knife was modelled on the knives imported from Solingen, with a wooden handle, large blade, screwdriver, can

Modern photograph of the first Soldier's Knife.

opener, and reamer. The project was not a success; the new Swiss knives were very good quality, but the German firms could always produce knives more cheaply in their factories than could Swiss craftsmen working from a series of small workshops. All of the other cutlers in the Association pulled out of the army project after a year, leaving Karl Elsener to struggle on. He lost his fortune and only avoided bankruptcy with the help of his relatives.

The Swiss Officer's Knife was patented on June 12, 1897.

Elsener persevered, throwing his energies into the development of other multi-purpose knives; the Schoolboys' Knife, the Cadet Knife, the Farmers' Knife, and in 1897 registered the design which was to make his fortune; the Officer's and Sports Knife. The design was similar to the Soldier's Knife, but lighter in weight and more elegant, with a smooth fiber handle, an additional small blade and a corkscrew. (Using only two springs for six tools).

Modern photograph of the first Officer's Knife.

The knife failed to impress the Swiss army establishment and was not included among the official equipment, but quickly became a success with the officers themselves, who saw the merits of the new design and chose to buy the knives from cutlery outlets.

The newly independent master cutler ran advertisements in the local newspapers to promote his specialities and to offer repair work and a daily honing service. Victoria, his mother, sold his products in the hat shop in the family home.

Cover of the 1903 price list of Karl Elsener's knife factory (Messer-Fabrik).

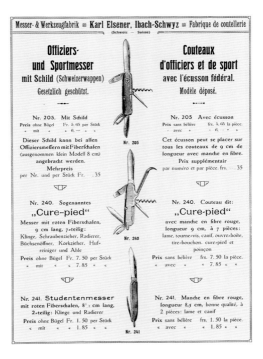

Messer- & Werkzeugfabrik ▬ **Karl Elsener, Ibach-Schwyz** ▬ Fabrique de coutellerie
(Schweiz — Suisse)

Offiziers- und Sportmesser
mit Schild (Schweizerwappen)
Gesetzlich geschützt.

Couteaux d'officiers et de sport
avec l'écusson fédéral.
Modèle déposé.

Nr. 205. Mit Schild
Preis ohne Bügel   Fr. 5, 65 per Stück
« mit   »   « 6, — « «

Dieser Schild kann bei allen
Offiziersmessern mit Fiberschalen
(ausgenommen klein Modell 8 cm)
angebracht werden.
Mehrpreis
per Nr. und per Stück Fr. —.35

Nr. 205

Nr. 205 Avec écusson
Prix sans bélière   frs. 5, 65 la pièce.
« avec   »   « 6, — « «

Cet écusson peut se placer sur
tous les couteaux de 9 cm de
longueur avec manche en fibre.
Prix supplémentaire
par numéro et par pièce. frs. —.35

Nr. 240. Sogenanntes
„Cure-pied"
Messer mit roten Fiberschalen,
9 cm lang, 7-teilig:
Klinge, Schraubenzieher, Radierer,
Büchsenöffner, Korkzieher, Huf-
reiniger und Ahle
Preis ohne Bügel Fr. 7.50 per Stück
« mit   « « 7.85 « «

Nr. 240

Nr. 240. Couteau dit:
„Cure-pied"
avec manche en fibre rouge,
longueur 9 cm, à 7 pièces:
lame, tourne-vis, canif, ouvre-boîte,
tire-bouchon. cure-pied et
poinçon
Prix sans bélière   frs. 7.50 la pièce.
« avec   » « 7.85 « «

Nr. 241. **Studentenmesser**
mit roten Fiberschalen, 8½ cm lang,
2-teilig: Klinge und Radierer
Preis ohne Bügel Fr. 1.50 per Stück
« mit   « « 1.85 « «

Nr. 241

Nr. 241. Manche en fibre rouge,
longueur 8,5 cm, bonne qualité, à
2 pièces: lame et canif
Prix sans bélière   frs. 1.50 la pièce.
« avec   » « 1.85 « «

Dual language (German and French) catalogue covering not only cutlery but pocket knives. Here three models—the Officer's and Sports Knife (205), Hoofcleaner for horsemen (240), and Student's (241). Note that the Swiss shield can be added to the Officer's Knife for a small extra cost.

The popularity of this knife prompted a flood of German imitations and Elsener could only retain his market through constant innovation and by ensuring that his knives were of the very highest quality. New models were produced with the addition of wood saws, scissors, tweezers, toothpicks and lanyard shackles. In 1909, 25 years after the start of his workshop, Elsener found the perfect way of distinguishing his original knives from the German imitations. From that year the Swiss government gave permission for Elsener to mark all his knives with the Swiss emblem, a cross, inlaid into the red fiber handle. In the same year Karl's mother died at the age of 73. In remembrance of her contribution as mother and business woman Karl took her name, Victoria, as his trademark.

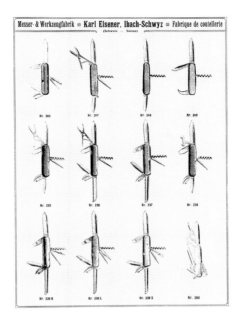

The expanding range of Karl Elsener's knives.

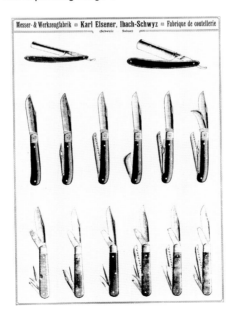

Cut-throat razors and another knife range from the catalogue.

Victoria

Victoria knives won many gold and silver awards in international exhibitions and became synonymous with Swiss quality and precision manufacturing.

The First World War period brought both opportunity and problems for the firm. Raw materials were hard to obtain from abroad, but the demand for soldier's knives and rifle parts increased and the shortfall of imports led to increased demand within Switzerland for all the firm's products.

The end of the war saw many changes. In 1918 Karl Elsener, the founder, died aged 58 leaving a thriving factory to his sons Carl and Alois. Prosperity was shortlived as the factory was plunged into crisis with the decline in demand for knives from the military, and the reopening of the domestic market to cheaper foreign competition. Victoria knives' reputation for quality was sustained and the Karl's sons struggled to keep the factory going. They were saved by the development of stainless steel. The process was discovered in 1921, and by 1923 Victoria knives were being produced in the new material. The French word *inoxydable* (stainless) was added to the company trademark, shortened to Inoxyd, and eventually incorporated into the comp-

Karl's son, Carl (1886-1950).

any name as Victorinox. There were problems associated with the introduction of the new stainless steel. Some knife collectors, even today, refuse to believe that stainless steel can ever achieve a really sharp cutting edge. However, the process has come a long way since the 1920s and 1930s. The high-carbon steels produced now can match any other material for hardness and cutting power.

CHAPTER 4

VICTORINOX AND SCHWYZ

A t the end of the 19th century, Schwyz would have seemed a very unlikely setting for the development of an internationally renowned cutlery business. Traveler's reports of the time describe the canton as one of magnificent green meadows, fruit orchards and sleepy villages. The main activity was agriculture, and in 1883 there were only 26 registered firms, with 1,700 employees between them. The largest firms in the area were a spinning mill in Ibach and a mechanized weaving and thread factory set up in 1880 in Kaltbach.

Tourism seemed the best hope for the region and was boosted by the construction of the St Gotthard railway and improvement of the road network. Some of the most splendid hotels in the world were built during the last years of the century around Lake Uri and Lake Lucerne. However, very few of the native population benefited from the growing tourist trade and most were exposed to the harsh realities of life. Jobs for workers and apprentices were scarce. Whereas in former centuries the young men of Schwyz had signed up as mercenaries in foreign conflicts, their only way out now was emigration and many set

The Schwyz basin with Cantonal capital at the foot of the Mythen.

Schwyz in the late 19th century. In the left foreground can be seen the home of Karl Elsener, with his first workshop beside it.

off in search of success to North America. Those left behind eked out a miserable existence, and there were many reports of beggars in the streets and highway robbers on the roads.

Karl Elsener's family were prosperous by local standards, with a felt and hat making factory established by 1849, to which a skin-processing works was added in 1893. Karl's first cutlery

The Elsener house in Ibach was divided into a cutlery workshop on the ground floor, apartments on the upper floors, and, in later years, a packing and mailing department on the first floor.

Provincial cutler's workshop, 19th century. Note the dog powering the grindstone! It's unlikely Karl Elsener's looked like this!

workshop in 1884 occupied the ground floor of an old forge, with several apartments in the upstairs rooms. In later years the packing and mailing department was set up on the first floor. The living room served also as an office for 43 years, right up until 1934.

At the turn of the century a working day spanned 11 hours. Every process was painstakingly done by hand; the only machines being the grindstones and polishing wheels that were driven by water power derived from the Tobelbach. Electric power was not available, so petrol lamps cast a meagre glow when daylight faded. The components for knives were fashioned from roughly stamped castings supplied by other firms. The various parts had to be precision filed in vices to fit and match each other exactly, so that the knife would function smoothly. They were then individually tempered, honed, polished and mounted.

Karl Elsener had to be workman, master craftsman and designer from the beginning, when he worked with one assistant. Apart from the quality of his workmanship, his other great gift was for a vision

In 1931 Brown Boveri et Cie installed the world's first fully electrical steel hardening shop in a new wing of the forge (far left of picture).

1909 and the firm's silver jubilee. Karl Elsener stands on the right in a leather smith's apron. His eldest son, Carl, is second from left.

This view shows the
expanded complex
from lower down the
slope.

sent to Ibach by indignant customers when they fail to live up to the
quality expected of Victorinox.

Although the original concept of the Swiss Army Knife remains
unchanged, the firm never forgot its founder's innovative approach and
improvements; new models and additions to the range of blades and
implements have been made throughout the product's history. One of
Karl Elsener's original aims was to bring much needed employment to
his home region. It is the proud boast of the company that, through
depression, war, and recession, they have been able to maintain a full
workforce, without having to lay off workers in troubled times. During
the 1950s, and 1960s it would have been possible for the company to
grow at a phenomenal rate. The demand for their knives throughout
the world was growing every year, and the only major complaints the
company received at this time were from customers frustrated at the
difficulty of obtaining the knives they wanted.

However, the company's mission was to maintain a stable, well
trained workforce and they feared that a sudden increase in production
would jeopardize both the quality of the product and the stability of
the company. Customers just had to wait until sales forecasts justified
the installation of new equipment and training of new workers. At this
time Victorinox did not even have a marketing department, and they
spent no money on paid advertising, relying only on word of mouth,

Carl Elsener (seated) and his son Carl Elsener Jr.

and editorial features to spread the fame of their product. There are few firms which have been able to maintain a reputation for the very highest level of quality for over 130 years. Victorinox's success has been due as much to the mutual trust between workforce and owners as to innovation and investment.

Victorinox Today

Today, with 950 employees, Victorinox is the largest industrial employer in the Canton of Schwyz and the largest cutlery manufacturer in Europe. At the factory in Ibach some 28,000 Swiss Army Knives are produced daily, along with 60,000 kitchen knives and 32,000 other pocket tools. Exports to over 120 countries take 90% of the production. The days of improvized workshops and offices in the family living room are long gone, with a complex of very modern factories and offices. The plant and 100 flats adjacent to it are heated using a pioneering system of heat recovery from the industrial processes. In some ways, though, the company still retains an old-fashioned view of business, with a highly skilled workforce, 10% of whom are employed in checking each knife as it leaves the factory, and a commitment to steady growth based on doing what they know best.

Polishing taking place in the Polishing Shop of the 1943 factory.

As part of their commitment to quality, the company have always offered a repair service for their knives, replacing any part which breaks or proves defective. A very small percentage of knives come back to the factory for repair within their first five years, but the Victorinox guarantee can cause problems with older knives. Customers become so attached to their knives that they will keep them for many years in constant use. Then, when springs are weakening with age, or a blade has been sharpened so many times that it almost wears away, they send the knife back for repair. In many cases it would be cheaper for Victorinox to replace the knife with a new model, but a well-used Swiss Army Knife has great sentimental value; the owner cannot bear to part with his trusted friend and insists on repair at any price.

The very high grade steel for the knives is not made in Switzerland. Stocks of steel are bought mostly from Bonpertuis in France and from Germany. Every other process in the production of the finished knives takes place in the factory at Ibach, using a relatively labor-intensive system. Some of the grinding and polishing of the blades is still performed by hand, by skilled cutlers. The best selling knives have to be assembled automatically, as so many are produced, but those models with special blade locks are still produced by hand.

Timeline of the Victorinox Company

1884 Karl Elsener I opens a cutler's workshop in Ibach-Schwyz.

1891 Karl Elsener I establishes the Association of Swiss Master Cutlers.

1897 The original Swiss Officer's and Sports is patented.

1909 Karl Elsener I uses his late mother's name Victoria as the brand name and registers the emblem with the cross and shield as a trademark.

1921 Following its invention, stainless steel (Inox) is used by the company; "Victoria" and "Inox" gives the name of the company and brand today—Victorinox.

1931 Carl Elsener II introduces automation to improve quality.

1945 The Swiss Army Knife becomes known all over the world. U.S. soldiers stationed in Europe buy it in large quantities and it begins to be a popular souvenir to take home.

1950 Carl Elsener III takes the company management into its third generation.

1979 "Messerfabrik Carl Elsener" is transformed into a family company.

1984 The company doubles its manufacturing and office space.

1989 Under its Swiss Army brand, Victorinox enters the North American watch business.

1992 Victorinox opens its first sales subsidiary in Japan.

1999 Victorinox enters the international travel gear market with the American TRG Group in St. Louis as the licensee.

2000 The Victorinox Foundation is established which holds 90% of the share capital of Victorinox AG.

2001 Victorinox launches a clothing line in the U.S. and opens the first Victorinox store in New York's Soho district, selling products from all five categories.

2005 Victorinox acquires the long-standing Swiss knife and

watch manufacturer Wenger SA in Delémont and allows it to operate as an independent subsidiary.

2007   Carl Elsener IV takes over the running of the business and further expands Victorinox.

2008   Victorinox opens the first Flagship store in Europe at New Bond Street, London.

2013   Wenger's knife business is incorporated into the Victorinox brand; Carl Elsener III dies.

2014   Victorinox acquires the travel gear business from previous licensee TRG Group and establishes the new business unit Victorinox Travel Gear AG. The company is celebrates its 130th anniversary.

2015   Victorinox advocates sustainably produced electricity; all electricity is drawn from local hydroelectric power plants.

2016   Victorinox team up with Nespresso to make a limited edition Swiss Army knife using recycled coffee capsules.

2017   Victorinox closed the apparel division to focus on other core product lines.

2018   Heating oil is used only in emergencies; waste heat is recovered from production to provide up to 75% of that needed by the operational buildings at the headquarters' location.

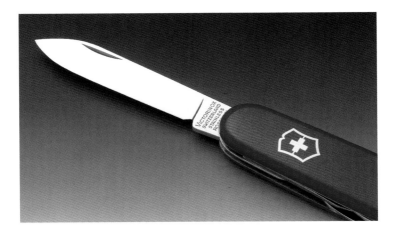

Schwyz Today

The Canton which gave Schwyz its name has come a long way since Karl Elsener decided to devote his energies to creating stable employment in the region. Tourism has developed from the luxury hotel trade of the 1890s to a thriving business providing a range of activities throughout the year, from watersports on the lakes to walking tours and winter sports.

The combination of tourism, agriculture, and industry give the people of Schwyz the kind of prosperity which would not have seemed possible in the 19th century, when young people were forced to leave their home country in search of work, or try to scrape a living working the land. Switzerland

The range of knives produced is extraordinary and growing all the time as new uses are identified; some of the latest novelties are kits designed specifically for in-line skaters, for mountain bikers, for golfers, and the Cyber Tool for computer and electronic enthusiasts. Victorinox has had strong links with the American market since the knives sold at PX stores and carried by American servicemen after the Second World War helped to spread the fame of the Swiss Army Knife throughout the world. The American domestic steel and cutlery

Switzerland in general—and Schwyz in particular—is breathtakingly beautiful as can be seen from these tourist photographs and those of the Victorinox building nestling under the mountains.

Victorinox is synonymous with Swiss Knife Valley and details can be found
at www.swissknifevalley.ch

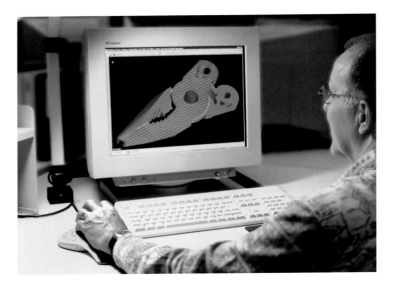

Computers are now used in the design process.

industry was developed by entrepreneurs and craftsmen from Britain, France, and Germany during the course of the 19th century.

Folding pocket knives have always formed a major part of their output, to cater for pioneers, huntsmen, and ranchers. Even today, there are many hundreds of companies and individual craftsmen making various kinds of pocket knife, so it is surprising that a knife from Switzerland should have taken such a firm hold on the market.

The Swiss Army knife has become a symbol of fine design and craftsmanship throughout the world and the company has built on this reputation with the development of other products. Victorinox Swiss Army brand watches have recently been introduced, combining the two precision products for which Swiss craftsmen have become justly famous.

The company acts as sponsor for many enterprises, including a hot air balloon team, sailing teams, a bob team, a sponsor of Bertrand Piccard's project "Solar Impulse"—around the world in a solar airplane—and some partnerships with tourism organizations.

Inevitably, Victorinox has been approached over the years by every conceivable kind of expedition, from mountaineers to polar explorers,

A symbol of fine design and craftsmanship throughout the world.

and they have the testimony of the participants that their Swiss Army Knives proved to be an indispensable part of the expedition's equipment. Recent formal sponsorships include the 37,797nm flight around North and South America by Gerard and Margi Moss.

Victorinox is still part-owned and managed by the Elsener family. The grandson of the founder, Karl Elsener Sr, is the senior managing director and has prepared the fourth generation of Elseners to take over the company. The factory in Ibach is known not only for the Swiss Army Knife, but for a range of domestic cutlery and professional chef's knives. As a family firm, Victorinox has been able through the years to keep to the philosophy of its founder through good times and bad, providing stable employment to the people of Schwyz. In a recent interview, Karl Elsener Sr outlined the firm's philosophy:

"It has always been the main goal at Victorinox to maintain jobs, and that is the way it will stay. Every person needs useful work and the opportunity to create meaning in their life. To offer workplaces is a contribution to the welfare of people. Everything else, even the quality of our products, serves this purpose."

CHAPTER 5

HOW THE KNIVES ARE MADE

Victorinox is, understandably, reluctant to allow too much photography within its manufacturing plant and too much detail on its manufacturing processes. Nevertheless, the photographs in this chapter show well the attention to detail and individual precision given to each Swiss Army Knife by the people who make them. The photographs on this page and page 61 show the individual components that go together to make two knives—the metal-covered Pioneer model and a red plastic version of the Spartan. Karl Elsener wanted not only business success, but also to bring employment to Schwyz and its neighborhood.

While much of the manufacturing process is automated, all the quality control and checking functions are carried out under the expert eye of a professional workforce.

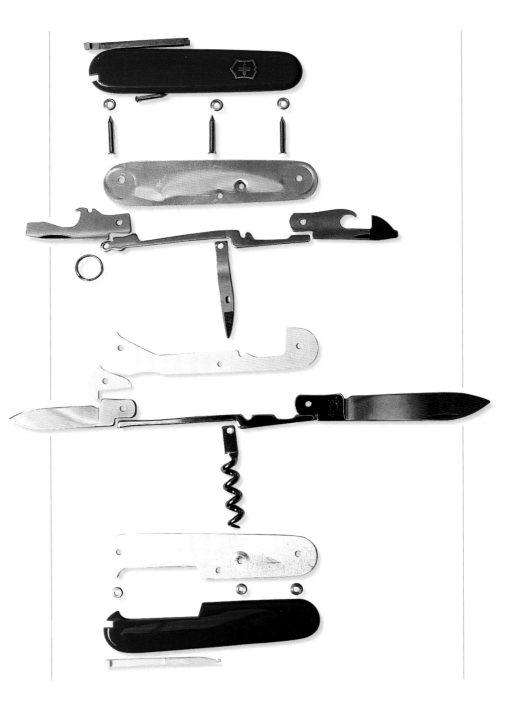

While much of the manufacturing process is automated, all the quality control and checking functions are carried out under the expert eye of a professional workforce.

CHAPTER 6

THE SWISSCHAMP AND THE CLASSIC

O ut of the many hundreds of knife models and variations available, the Classic and the SwissChamp are among the most popular. These two knives typify the range and incorporate most of the features available in different configurations within the other knives on the market. In addition to the technical details and official descriptions of each of the blades and tools, some examples are given of the way in which some of these have been used by Swiss Army Knife owners who have written in to Victorinox with their stories.

If you have owned one of these knives for more than five minutes, you will instantly be able to give half a dozen other uses for the tools, as their use is limited only by the imagination of the owner. However, it is sad to say that not a single authenticated report could be found of any of the SwissChamp's tools being used for the traditional "picking stones out of horses' hoofs." The closest was an incidence of the pliers being used to pick a splinter out of an elephant's foot. Another stereotype bites the dust…

OPPOSITE: The distinctive trademarks of the Victorinox knives: Swiss emblem and trademark on knife blade—above, the form until 2007; below, since then.

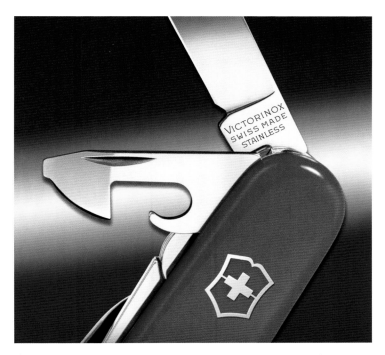

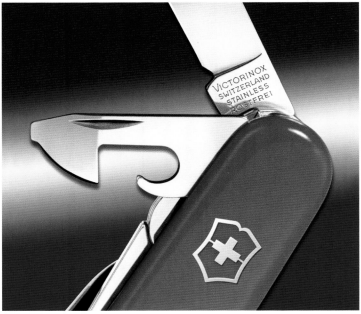

Technical Specifications

The blades in all the knives are made from a special stainless chrome molybdenum steel, mixed from carbon, chrome, molybdenum, manganese, and silicon. Through a hardening process at 1,900°F (and an annealing temperature of 140°F) the cutting blades achieve a hardness of RC 56. (A cheap blade would register less than 50 on the standard hardness scale.) This is too hard to be sharpened with steel, so a carborundum stone has to be used. Different degrees of hardness are required for the various tools. The wood saw, scissors and nail files have a hardness of RC 53, the screwdrivers, tin openers and awls RC 52, and the corkscrew and springs RC 49.

The pressure exerted by the springs has to be finely balanced to allow efficient operation and prevent closure during use, while still enabling the user to open the knife smoothly. The spring exerts a pressure of 26.5lb on the large blade and 17.6lb on the small blade. These combine to exert 44lb of pressure on the corkscrew. With two springs and six pressure locations a total of 154lb pressure is achieved. In the case of the SwissChamp model, with eight springs and 24 pressure points, a total of 600lb is achieved.

The separators have been made from aluminum alloy (known as Alox) since 1951, making the knife much lighter. Formerly these separating layers between the tools were made from nickel-silver. The rivets in the knives are made from brass and the outer casing (known as scales) from Cellidor, a hard-wearing material made in the USA.

The SwissChamp

The SwissChamp was first introduced in 1985—since then it has been generally recognized as the best model in the line up; it is billed as the knife that has everything. Considerable ingenuity and a process of evolution over more than 100 years have produced a tool which is equipped for almost any situation you are likely to encounter. Prized by explorers, adventurers, and sportsmen, the Champ has traveled to virtually every part of the globe, above and below water level. The SwissChamp is available in many colors, including transparent silver, red, black, red translucent, blue translucent, with rosewood handles, genuine horn handles, genuine staghorn, genuine mother of pearl, and hardwood handles (rustic look). The closed knife measures 3.6in and weighs 6.5oz. The official list of features gives 31 functions from 64 components, all tightly packed into eight layers.

	Large blade
	Small blade
	Corkscrew
	Can opener with Screwdriver 3mm
	Bottle opener with Screwdriver 6mm with Wire stripper
	Punch reamer and sewing awl
	Key ring
	Tweezers
	Toothpick
	Scissors
	Multipurpose hook
	Wood saw
	Fish scaler with Hook disgorger with 18. Ruler—inches and cm
	Nail file with Metal file with Nail cleaner with Metal saw
	Screwdriver 2.5mm
	Chisel 4mm
	Pliers with Wire cutter with Wire crimping tool
	Phillips screwdriver 1/2
	Ballpoint pen
	Magnifying glass
	Mini screwdriver
	Stainless steel pin

The Large Blade

The strength of the spring ensures that this remains stable in use, and the blade remains exceptionally sharp for a long period of time. Victorinox does supply carborundum stone sharpeners, as the blades cannot be sharpened with steels. "A group of hikers on the Hawaiian Island of Kauai became stranded on a spit of land in the middle of a fast-flowing river. They escaped by cutting through bamboos five inches in

diameter with the large blade of a Victorinox knife and jamming the poles between boulders as handrails while they crossed to the river bank."

The Small Blade

Useful for more intricate tasks, but just as sharp and tough as the large blade. "A Canadian working in Germany prevented a railroad accident when the barrier to stop traffic from crossing the track jammed as a train was approaching. He inserted the small blade of his Swiss Army Knife into the barrier mechanism and lowered the barrier just as the train sped through."

Corkscrew

This was one of the extra features added to the original Soldier's Knife to form the Officer's Knife. The success of the Officer's Knife led to all the subsequent refinements, and it may have been the corkscrew which tipped the balance. After all, being the

only person in the regiment who carries a corkscrew at all times must put you in a considerable position of power.

Can Opener

The best can opener available in a pocket knife, with a design patented by Victorinox in 1951. There was a can opener on the original Soldier's knife, but it took strength and practice to use; anyone can use this new model. "In 1998 a guest on a German TV show *Wetten, dass?* (in English "You bet...") bet that he could open ten tins faster using a Swiss Army Knife than an opponent using an electric tin opener. He won."

Screwdriver 3mm

The tip of the can opener is a useful screwdriver, suitable for small slotted screws as well as Phillips screws. "At a concert in Sydney a pencil fell into the Steinway grand, causing clunky notes. When the pianist, conductor, and choristers had all failed to retrieve it, a member of the audience produced a Swiss Army Knife, unscrewed the front cover of the piano and restored harmony."

Bottle Opener

The first bottle opener was introduced in 1942 and was a popular feature with the US servicemen who bought the knife and spread its popularity round the world after the Second World War.

Screwdriver 6mm

The head of the bottle opener forms a large screwdriver for slotted screws. This feature is specially designed to prevent it from closing in use. It is aligned behind the main axis of the knife, the tip is positioned at 89º (to it, and the spring applies extra pressure to hold it in place.

Wire Stripper

A sharp edge for stripping small wires.

Punch Reamer and Sewing Awl

Another of the original features of the Soldier's Knife. At that time it was used for repairs to leather harness or equipment. The sharp edge can cut precisely to create a smooth-edged opening in many materials or to drill into wood. Most hard materials can be pierced with this sharp, tough point. "A British army officer returning from an expedition in the South Seas reports that the punch is ideal for knocking the eyes out of the coconuts which formed a staple part of their diet."

Keyring

This fitting replaced the old lanyard shackle in 1968. The SwissChamp may be too large to use as a conventional keyring, but the attachment is essential for climbers, sailors, and workmen needing to attach their knife to belts or equipment so that it is always to hand.

Tweezers

Introduced along with the wood saw in 1902, presumably to remove the splinters that can result from wood-working.

Toothpick

The plastic material now used for the toothpick is a lot more pleasant to use than the 1902 metal version.

Both toothpick and tweezers can be replaced as individual items.

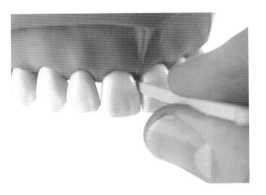

Scissors

Scissors have been included in the knives since 1902. The springs can wear out if used extensively—but they are easy to replace and can be bought separately.

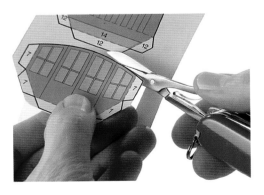

Multipurpose Hook

This has proved a popular addition to the knife since 1991. Uses range from opening sardine tins to carrying heavy parcels.

Wood Saw

All the teeth in this saw are ground, ensuring a sharp cutting edge. The wood saw has been included in the knives since 1902. "An archaeologist from Argentina ran into a snowstorm on a lonely mountain road, without food or water. His car became stuck in the snow, but he was able, with the saw on his SwissChamp, to cut a tree branch strong enough to use as a lever to free his car from the snowdrift."

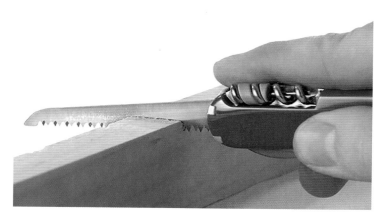

Fish Scaler and Hook Disgorger

An unusually specific designation for a multi-purpose knife, but this scaler, first developed in 1952, really does the job better than a conventional knife or scraper. This was the only blade for which Chris Bonington could find no use on his Himalayan expedition "there being a distinct shortage of freshwater fish half way up Annapurna's south face."

Ruler–Inches and Centimetres

The ruler is marked off in centimetres on one side and in inches on the other.

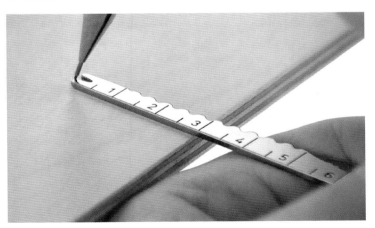

Metal File

The reverse of the nail file has a hard, chrome-plated finish. The material from which the file is made is harder than conventional steel, so ideal for smoothing rough edges.

Metal Saw

The edge has an extra-hard finish and should cut through most metals.

Nail Cleaner

A step up from cleaning nails with the tip of the knife, which must have been the practice before this extra tool was included.

Nail File

A refinement introduced in 1952.

Screwdriver 2.5mm

One of five screwdrivers within the knife, which should provide enough variation in size and shape to tackle almost any screw.

Chisel 4mm

Included since 1985, the chisel can be used even with very hard woods to make precise cuts and grooves. "A French holiday maker describes how he and his family had

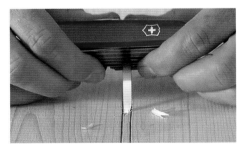

forgotten to pack any games for their stay on Ile de Ré. During the first week of the holiday he fashioned an entire chess set from logs, using the saw, blades, and chisel of his son's Swiss Army knife."

Pliers and Wire Cutter

Ridged for extra grip, these are strong enough to cope with anything that a full sized pair of pliers can tackle.

"During an expedition to a remote part of West Nepal, one of the expedition elephants got a sharp piece of bamboo in her foot. The medical officer borrowed Colonel John Blashford's Swiss Army knife and extracted the splinter with the pliers." A member of the film crew for *Little Buddha* reports that he performed two emergency dental extractions using the pliers while they were filming in a remote part of Bhutan!

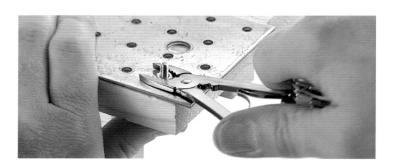

Phillips Screwdriver

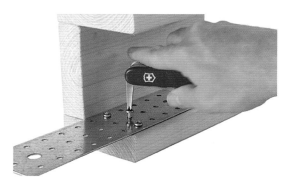

Introduced in 1952, when Phillips screws became widely used. Will fit many sizes of screw head.

Magnifying Glass

A powerful magnifier with toughened lens. "A traveler in South Australia was on a bus when a bee flew in and stung a girl who was allergic to bee stings. With his magnifier he checked that the poison sac had not emptied its contents, then removed it using the tweezers."

Mini Screwdriver

This is a really ingenious design, patented in 1983. The base of the screwdriver fits into the corkscrew. It is fine enough to deal with intricate electrical connections or with the really tiny screws on the side arms of spectacles.

Wire Crimping Tool

This can be used for closing up wires crimps, such as those used on some fishing tackle rigs.

Biro

Last—but not least—a means of writing, if only for an explorer's last words!

If further proof is needed of the adaptability of the SwissChamp, it surely comes in this letter from Thomas R. Black, an American who moved from Texas to Siberia for a two year stay in 1993:

"Among hundreds of uses, I used it to install a door alarm, to slice the hard Russian bread daily and spread the butter when I could find it, to tighten the hinges on my doors and the faucets on my sink. Additionally it was used to pry open a sticky car door, to carve a walking stick, to punch holes in leather for the saddle I assembled to go on a riding trip, to open bottles and cans, to adjust radio antennas, to start a fire on a camping trip (with the magnifier), to skin a fish and a rabbit, to clean out the cracks between floorboards, to strip some insulated wire when I installed my own phone, to open and repair my laptop, to cut rope for a clothesline, to pound nails, to pick the tough Russian meat from between my teeth, to clip my fingernails, to cut fabric, to drill a hole in the apartment door (solid oak) to install a small "peep hole," as an aid in re-stringing a tennis racket, to peel a thousand potatoes and much, much more."

The Classic

The simplest of the knives, with just two layers of blades, this is the natural successor to the original Soldier's knife. The Classic is the most popular knife of all for consumers and as promotional gifts. The standard size is just 58mm (2.3in) long, 15g (0.7oz) in weight, so it serves well as part of a keyring. Classics are produced

The Classic SD: note the screwdriver head on the nail file.

in a wide range of colors and finishes apart from the traditional Swiss Army red, including flags of the world, fashion and pastel colors, genuine horn, rosewood and polished or hammered silver. The most basic models do not incorporate the screwdriver head with the nail file—those with the screwdriver are known as "Classic SD" models.

Another small knife, the MiniChamp; it also produced with an LED flashlight and 16 functions—the Midnite MiniChamp.

The Classic Transparent series includes the Signature and Signature Lite.

CHAPTER 7

THE VICTORINOX FAMILY

Since Karl Elsener's design for the Soldier's Knife in 1891, the knives have been through a continuous process of evolution and refinement. New tools have been introduced regularly to reflect the changing needs of users. One also suspects that the designers in Ibach have had some fun over the years dreaming up new uses for existing tools and trying to fit ever more implements into the smallest space possible. If it were possible to produce a solar powered traveling iron which would fold neatly into the SwissChamp we can be sure that it would have been included.

The Timeline of the Swiss Soldier's Knife

1891	Wooden scales with blade, punch, tin opener, screwdriver; 5oz
1908	Fiber scales with Swiss emblem embossed (not white) 4.4oz
1951	Fiber scales with Swiss emblem embossed (not white) 3.2oz
1954	Fiber with bushings, with Swiss emblem embossed (not white) 3.2oz
1961	Alox red with Swiss emblem embossed (not white) 2.5oz
1965	Alox silver color with Swiss emblem embossed (not white) 2.5oz
1980	Alox silver color with Swiss emblem in white on red
1994	Regular instead of tubular rivet
2003	New German Army knife issued
2009	The Soldier Knife 08 was first issued to the Swiss Armed Forces

The first Soldier's knife contained just one large blade, a screwdriver, can opener, and reamer, which also served as a punch. The handle was finished in wood, which had a tendency to crack with time. Elsener's breakthrough, and the saving of his overstretched company, came with his perception that a more sophisticated knife would appeal to the military as part of their personal kit, not supplied by the army. Using the Soldier's Knife as his model, he worked out how he could put extra blades on the back of the knife, using the same springs as the blades on the front, thus adding more utensils without increasing the size of the handle. On June 12, 1897, he registered the design for the Officer's Knife which has been the blueprint for all the company's subsequent products.

Swiss Army Knife owners today would instantly recognize the original Officer's knife, with its distinctive red handle and compact design, despite the missing Swiss emblem. Only a small blade and corkscrew were added to the Soldier's Knife components to transform it into an Officer's Knife, but these, together with the lighter weight and more comfortable, durable handle, proved to be exactly what the military and the general public wanted. In the early literature of the company the name "Officer's Knife" is always printed in inverted commas to make the point that this knife was never adopted by the armed forces as part of routine personal kit issued to each soldier or officer.

However, the popularity of the design was such that both officers and soldiers in the Swiss army bought the knife privately and used it as part of their day-to-day equipment. The Swiss army continued to issue the standard Soldier's Knife, but from 1893 Elsener was no longer the exclusive Swiss supplier. A rival company, Paul Boechat & Cie, submitted a tender to supply knives to the same specification as the Elsener knife and, thereafter, the two companies shared the contract.

Boechat became Fabrique Suisse de Courtetelleries et Services, then was acquired by Theodore Wenger and renamed Wenger & Cie. With Elsener in the German-speaking canton of Schwyz and Wenger in the French-speaking Jura region, rivalry was intense. In 1908 the Swiss government decided to avoid friction between the two growing companies by using each supplier for half of its requirements. A new

The Timeline of the 3.5"
"Swiss Army Officer's Knife"

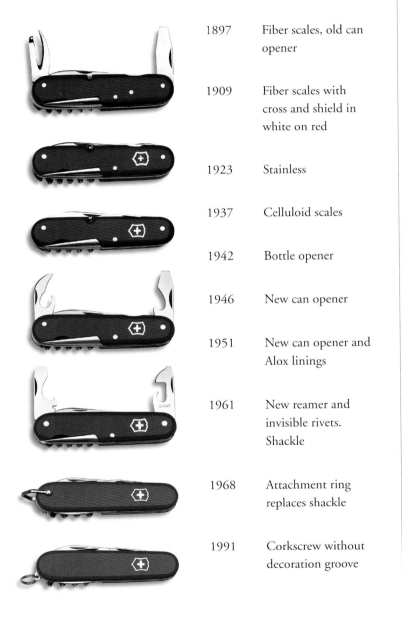

1897	Fiber scales, old can opener
1909	Fiber scales with cross and shield in white on red
1923	Stainless
1937	Celluloid scales
1942	Bottle opener
1946	New can opener
1951	New can opener and Alox linings
1961	New reamer and invisible rivets. Shackle
1968	Attachment ring replaces shackle
1991	Corkscrew without decoration groove

specification was issued, with lighter, tougher fiber scales to replace the old wooden ones and the two companies have been supplying the Swiss army ever since. By a gentlemen's agreement the two rival companies have agreed that Wenger should use for their advertising the phrase "Genuine Swiss Army Knives," while Victorinox use the slogan, "The Original Swiss Army Knife."

Despite its failure to be adopted by the army, Elsener's Officer's Knife was selling well through retail outlets in Switzerland direct from the workshops at Ibach. Modifications were made to the design and in 1902 new models were issued containing a wood saw, scissors, and the ingenious tweezers and toothpick now contained in most of the modern knives.

Although the knives were made from the finest steel available at the time, they were inevitably prone to rust with age and exposure to moisture. A major change came about in 1923 with the first knives to use the newly invented stainless steel, and new developments in plastics prompted the change in 1937 to Cellidor "scales"—the colored plates covering the handle of the knife. The Soldier's Knife continued to be supplied with fiber scales until 1961. Up to this point the well equipped Swiss officer would have been able to open cans, saw timber for firewood, take the splinters out of his fingers with the tweezers, cut his food, open his wine, clean his teeth, carry out repairs to his kit with the screwdriver and reamer, trim his beard and cut his nails with the scissors, and open letters from home with the small blade. He would always be able to find his knife, thanks to the lanyard shackle added in 1902. But, to be honest, the can opener would have taken some skill to use efficiently, a beer drinker would have had to use some ingenuity to take the cap off a bottle and the poor man was still cleaning his nails with the edge of his knife. By the time the Victorinox knives went on sale in the American PX stores just after the Second World War, they had solved all these problems with an improved design for the can opener (patented in 1946), a bottle cap lifter, nail file, and nail cleaner

During the 1950s Alox (aluminum alloy) linings between the blades replaced the nickel silver linings, giving a smoother and more durable mechanism and reducing the overall weight; wire strippers, and benders were introduced and the designers perfected a Phillips screwdriver, as this type of screw grew in popularity. The specific needs of sportsmen and explorers were also addressed with the introduction of a custom-made fish scaler and hook disgorger. From 1961, the Soldier's Knife was supplied with Alox scales, reducing the weight of the knife to 2.3oz.

During the 1960s and 1970s, demand for Victorinox knives grew at a phenomenal rate and production, spread between workshops which had grown up around the original site, could barely keep pace with demand. The knives attained a scarcity value and it was at this time that many of the stories about miraculous escapes and rescues using only a Swiss Army Knife started to appear in the newspapers. Inevitably this shortage of the original articles prompted a dramatic increase in the number of imitations appearing on the market throughout the world. Many of these cheaper copies incorporated a white cross on the handles and both Victorinox and Wenger had to spend time and resources protecting their reputations through international copyright law. Even today, Victorinox include in their promotional literature the caveat that buyers should always look at the base of the large blade for the words "Victorinox Switzerland" to ensure that the knife they are buying is an original Swiss Army Knife.

A new state-of-the-art factory and office building was opened early in the 1980s and freed the company not only to increase production of its most popular lines, but also to expand the range and respond to a new range of consumers. One of the most ingenious additions of this time was the patented mini-screwdriver, designed to fit on to the end of the corkscrew and fine enough to use with the screws on the hinge of a pair of spectacles.

The Swiss Army Knife attained the status of a cult in the USA and Europe through a popular television series, *MacGyver*. Richard Dean Anderson played the role of the laid-back former Special Forces Agent, who specialized in saving the world from villains, spies, mad scientists and psychopaths. MacGyver, unusually, never carried a gun and relied on his trusty "SAK" to extricate him from every impossible situation. In the course of the series, from 1985 to 1994 MacGyver used his Swiss Army Knife for every conceivable purpose, from picking locks to defusing bombs. The product could not have had a more effective form of advertising. Children and teenagers throughout America had to have their own "SAK" so that they could be prepared for anything in the woods or playground. The series was also a great success in France and Germany, where demand for Victorinox knives became far greater than the production capabilities of the factory. The infinite number of uses for the Swiss Army Knife, as demonstrated by MacGyver, gave every American adult the excuse to regard their (relatively expensive) purchase as a necessity rather than a luxury "toy" for the city-dweller.

The Time Keeper

During the champagne years of the 1980s the market for business gadgets really took off. Instead of using the fixed facilities of home or office, business people had to have their own personal equipment, and it was all getting smaller. Computerized personal organizers, laptop computers, mobile phones, portable CD, and tape recorders encouraged the idea of the fullyequipped executive on the move, ready for anything. But there are some things that a computer chip cannot do—and a Swiss Army Knife can. Far from superseding the 100-year old "portable workbox," this trend increased demand for the knives and for new "executive" models. In 1985, a ballpoint pen and fine screwdriver for mending glasses were added to the range of tools. The company also saw the potential for modifying the Swiss Army Knife so that it would form a portable DIY toolkit. Pliers and a chisel were added to the standard knives, and a new Swiss Tool was introduced, equipped with 23 functions, including a ruler and full range of screwdriver heads. A new range of knives was also produced with a handle shaped to improve the grip and a locking device for the main blade so that it cannot close even under extreme pressure.

Special kits including the knives have been produced to cater for the needs of particular activities, including the Mountain Biker's kit, and In-line Skater's kit, and an all-purpose Survival kit. In 1990, Victorinox took the logical step of combining the two precision products for which Switzerland is renowned; a knife was produced with a Swiss watch built into the handle, and now they have their own range of Victorinox watches.

Although the company now produces a huge range of products, the best-sellers world-wide are still the Standard, the Huntsman, the SwissChamp, and the many versions of the Classic knife. Second in the list of their current best-sellers, though, is the SwissCard. This is the first radical move away from Karl Elsener's original design—but although ideal for the office-bound executive, it is unlikely that this new shape will take over from the Swiss Army Knife as we know it. Like the bicycle, Elsener's design has an elegant simplicity and fitness for purpose that has not been bettered in over 100 years.

The Time Keeper (1991–2006)

The Timeline of the Victorinox Swiss Army Knife

1884   January 1, Karl Elsener starts his own business.

1891   The Swiss army is supplied with the sturdy soldier's knife for the first time.

1897   Official registration of the Officer's Knife with extra small blade and corkscrew.

1902   New models with additional wood saw, scissors, tweezers, toothpick and shackle.

1909   Metal Swiss cross inlaid on the red fiber handles.

1923   The Swiss army knife made from stainless steel.

1937   Handles made from Cellidor replace fiber handles.

1942   New screwdriver with cap lifter, nail file with nail cleaner (on the back of the knife).

1946   New patented can opener.

1951   Improved can opener with small screwdriver, Alox dividers, new screwdriver, wire stripper, and bender.

1952   Phillips screwdriver forged with cut nail file, fish scaler with hook disgorger, metal saw, and metal file with nail file, and nail cleaner.

1957   Tweezer grip made from aluminum (previously nickel silver).

1961   New reamer with cutting edge, invisible rivets.

1968   Keyring replaces shackle.

1973   Magnifying glass and Phillips screwdriver, new shape small blade.

1975   New scissor spring (V-shaped).

1977   Small screwdriver (on the back of the knife).

1978   Tweezer grip made from plastic.

1980   Inlay made from stainless steel instead of nickel silver, new round Phillips screwdriver.

1983   Patented mini screwdriver stored within corkscrew.

1985   Ballpoint pen, small screwdriver (new shape), chisel, reamer with sewing eye, cap lifter with 90° lock.

1986	Pliers with wire cutter, combination tool with: cap lifter, can opener, screwdriver and wire stripper.
1987	Camouflage handles.
1990	Swiss watch in handle, new scissor spring with cam, scissors with guiding groove.
1991	Multi-purpose hook and pin, scissors riveted (previously screwed).
1992	Golfer blade, spatula, Phillips screwdriver (round), new without slot.
1994	Matt nylon handles for EcoLine, corkscrew without decorating groove.
1995	Wire crimping tool on pliers.
1998	Multi-purpose hook also with nail file.
1999	Wrench and bit holder, translucent handles.
2000	Altimeter electronics.
2001	Voyager electronics, new handle for small tweezers, toothpick, and ballpoint pen.
2002	Piezo lighter (until 2005), LED module plus new Phillips screwdriver.
2003	StayGlow (fluorescent handles).
2004	Plastic magnifying glass, blade shank 2.0mm instead of 2.4mm.
2005	Traveler electronics stainless, metal file ground, new stamping on blade shank.
2006	The SwissChamp XAVT released consisting of 118 parts and 80 functions.
2008	The Parachutist discontinued.
2009	Optional Pocket-Clip offered on the Sentinel.
2010	Presentation Master model released including a laser pointer, and detachable flash drive with fingerprint reader.
2011	The Tradesman discontinued.
2013	Cheese Knife produced.
2016	The Rucksack model replaced by the Forester.
2017	111mm product line revised; production of slide-lock models ceased.

Victorinox in the New Millennium

Victorinox acquired Wenger—the other manufacturer of Swiss Army Knives, in April 2005. A decision was made to keep both brands, although production has been merged to keep costs down. Since then, it has become the sole supplier of multi-purpose knives to the Swiss army, and has become the biggest manufacturer of pocket knives in the world.

Victorinox has had to keep up with the times by altering its products in line with changes in society. The most overt of these is the way that the aftermath of 9-11 has led to travel regulations in most countries which no longer allow one to fly with a pocket knife. In a similar vein, where red laser pointers used to be included on certain models, an ever-increasing pressure to de-risk commercial products has forced the company to remove them. In most places they have been replaced by white LED flashlights.

As with so many similar design icons—such as Zippo and Swatch, increased color variety and overall attractiveness both in the knives themselves as well their packaging has significantly increased collectability. This, in turn, has led to more Limited Editions being produced.

In recent years, Victorinox has diversified into many other product areas, including the creation of the Victorinox Travel Gear division, which produces and markets things like suitcases and backpacks. A foray into apparel was not considered successful, so in 2017 this division was closed.

The prevalence of electronic devices, from mobile phones to computers of every shape and size has led to a requirement for carrying / storing data, as well as for being able to work on the devices themselves. In answer to the former of these needs, Victorinox has produced several models which feature a high speed USB memory stick—these include the Midnite Manager@work, the Victorinox@work, and the Jetsetter@work. The latter is answered by the CyberTool, which is designed to provide technicians with the tools they need to strip and repair "any kind of IT gadget."

The Product Families

Victorinox product lines are divided into five categories:
• Swiss Army Knives
• Cutlery
• Watches
• Travel Gear
• Fragrances

Then further subdivided into the following groups:
• Small Pocket Knives
• Medium Pocket Knives
• Large Pocket Knives
• Swiss Tools
• Sport Tools
• SwissCards

Small Pocket Knives

The smallest knives produced by Victorinox are designed to be the perfect companion for everyday life, being practical, light and discreet. As such, they can be kept in the pocket, on a belt, or attached to your keys. Despite their diminutive size, they are high-quality items engineered for years of use, with specially alloyed and hardened blades that ensure the stainless steel tool edges retain their sharpness. There are 27 basic models in this category, however, there are lots of color variations to choose from.

Escort	Mini Champ Alox
Classic Alox	Midnite Mini Champ
Rally	Jetsetter@work Alox
Classic	Victorinox@work
Classic SD	Midnite Manager@work
Signature	Executive 81
Signature Lite	Executive Wood 81
Swiss Lite	Nail Clip 582
Jetsetter	Nail Clip 580
Rambler	Nail Clip Wood 580
Manager	Ambassador
Midnite Manager	Money Clip
Classic with Gold Ingot 1 Gram	Executive
Mini Champ	

Classic Alox

Key Features
Item number 0.6221.26
Collection Alox
High-grade Alox scales
1. Blade
2. Nail file with
3. Screwdriver 2.5mm
4. Scissors
5. Key ring

Dimensions
Height 0.2in
Length 2.3in
Weight 0.6oz

The Classic Alox is a small pocket knife which features Alox scales—it is designed to provide basic functionality in a package with the minimum dimensions.

Midnite Manager@work

The Midnite Manager@work is a small pocket knife is a truly multifunctional item that not only provides ten practical mechanical functions, but also features a pivoted and removable 16 GB USB memory stick as well as an LED flashlight.

Key Features

Item number 4.6336.TG16
1. Blade
2. Scissors
3. Nail file
4. Screwdriver
5. Bottle opener
6. Magnetic Phillips screwdriver
7. Wire stripper
8. USB Stick 3.0/3.1
9. Key ring
10. LED
11. Pressurized ballpoint pen

USB stick 16 GB
Interface: USB stick
3.0 Type-A / 3.1 Type-C
Read speed: 115 MB/s
Write speed: 25 MB/s

Dimensions
Height 0.7in
Length 2.3in
Weight 1.6oz.
Scale material ABS / Cellidor
Lockable blade No
One-hand blade No

Jetsetter@work Alox

The new Jetsetter@work Alox is another small pocket knife that features a pivoted and removable 16 GB 3.0/3.1 USB stick; it also provides six practical mechanical functions.

Key Features
Item number 4.6261.26G16B1
Collection Alox
1. Scissors
2. Bottle opener
3. Wire stripper
4. Phillips screwdriver 0/1,
   magnetic
5. Key ring
6. USB stick 3.0 / 3.1
   Interface: USB stick
   3.0 Type-A / 3.1 Type-C

Read speed: 115 MB/s
Write speed: 25 MB/s

Dimensions
Net weight 1oz
Height 0.7in
Length 2.3in
Weight 1oz
Scale material Alox
Lockable blade No
One-hand blade No

Classic with Gold Ingot 1 Gram

The Classic with Gold Ingot 1 Gram is a small pocket knife that is aimed at the discerning gentleman traveler who seeks a combination of elegance and practicality. Not only does it have eight mechanical functions, but it also features a one-gram ingot of gold inlaid into the side. All in all, it is a true collector's item.

Key Features	Dimensions
Item number 0.6203.87	Height 0.4in
1. Scissors	Length 2.3in
2. Tools	Weight 0.8oz
3. Tweezers	Scale material ABS / Cellidor
4. Small blade	Size 2in
5. Scissors	Lockable blade No
6. Nail file	One-hand blade No
7. Nail cleaner	
8. Key ring	

NailClip Wood 580

The NailClip Wood 580 is, as the name would suggest, a small pocket knife that features a nail clipper. This has a quick-release mechanism to make it easy to use, and the knife itself also has a nail file and a nail cleaner which combine to make it just as practical an item in the wilderness as in the office.

Key Features
Item number 0.6461.63
Collection Wood
1. Nail clipper
2. Key ring
3. Nail file
4. Nail cleaner
5. Small blade
6. Serrated edge scissors

Dimensions
Height 0.8in
Length 2.6in
Weight 1.3oz
Scale material Walnut wood
Lockable blade No
One-hand blade No
NailClip Wood 580

Money Clip Alox

The Money Clip Alox is a small pocket knife that features a handy money clip, making it act as both a wallet and a Swiss Army Knife. The main body has five mechanical functions with polished Alox scales on the sides.

Key Features
Item number 0.6540.16
Collection Alox
1. Large blade
2. Scissors
3. Nail file
4. Nail cleaner
5. Money clip

Dimensions
Height 0.3in
Length 2.9in
Weight 1oz
Scale material Alox
Lockable blade No
One-hand blade No

Classic SD

The Classic is the archetypal Swiss Army Knife—being both small and packed with seven useful functions, it is constructed of high quality stainless steel and made with Victorinox's renowned Swiss precision. There are enough variants—Limited Editions and different scale graphics in this one model alone to keep a collector busy for life!

Key Features
Item number 0.6223
1. Blade
2. Nail file with screwdriver
3. Scissors
4. Key ring
5. Tweezers
6. Toothpick

Dimensions
Height 0.4in
Length 2.3in
Weight 0.8oz
Scale material ABS/Cellidor
Lockable blade No
One-hand blade No

Medium Pocket Knives

The Original Swiss Army Knife—patented by Victorinox founder Karl Elsener on July 12, 1897, was the elegant, lightweight and exceptionally versatile Officer's and Sports Knife. Today this iconic knife—which is considered to belong in the "Medium" size category, is exhibited in museums all over the world, including New York's Museum of Modern Art and the International Design Museum in Munich, Germany. The Original Swiss Army Knife has become an established classic—synonymous with creativity, functionality and of course unparalleled Swiss quality. Other medium-sized knives include:

My First Victorinox
My First Victorinox H
Victorinox I Swiss Army Knives
Bantam and Bantam Alox
Walker
Cadet Alox
Recruit
Waiter
Sportsman
Tourist
Excelsior
Baker's Knife
Watchmaker 60
Watchopener
the Evolution series (S101, 10,
   Wood 10, 14, Wood 14, 17,
   Wood 17, S52, 11, 18, 23,
   S557, Wood S557, 28, S54
Junior 03 and Junior 09
Cigar 36 and Cigar 79
Compact
Spartan and Spartan Lite
Camper
Angler

Climber
Huntsman and Huntsman Lite
Traveller-Set
Mountaineer Ranger Handyman
Explorer
Tinker Small, Tinker, Super
   Tinker and Deluxe Tinker
Hiker
Fieldmaster
Fisherman
Swiss Champ, Wood Swiss
   Champ, Swiss Champ XLT,
   Swiss Champ XAVT
Cyber Tool S 1.7605.T,
   M 1.7725.T, L 1.7775.T,
   Lite 1.7925.T
Traveller and Traveller Lite
Expedition Kit
Swiss Army 1, Swiss Army 2,
   Swiss Army 6, Swiss Army 7
Electrician
Pioneer and Pioneer X
Farmer

Evolution Wood S557

The Evolution Wood S557 is a medium pocket knife that has ergonomically shaped wooden scales to provide a firm grip which have the Victorinox logo engraved into them. Designed to be used for a wide range of adventure activities, it features 18 functions including a locking main blade.

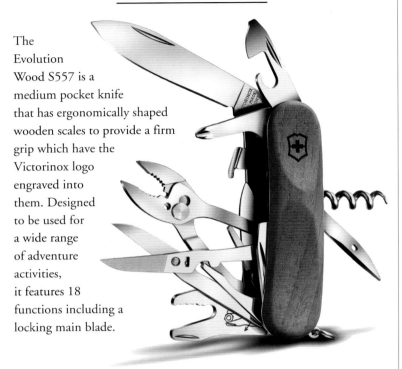

Key Features
Item number 2.5221.S63
Collection Wood
1. Lock blade
2. Nail file
3. Nail cleaner
4. Serrated edge scissors
5. Can opener
6. Small screwdriver
7. Bottle opener
8. Lockable screwdriver
9. Wire cutter
10. Lockable Phillips screwdriver
11. Adjustable opening pliers

12 Wire crimper inside-outside
13 Wire stripper
14 Nut wrench
15 Universal wrench M3, M4, M5
16. Corkscrew
17. Punch reamer
18. Key ring

Dimensions
Height 1.1in
Length 3.3in
Weight 4.5oz

Spartan

The Spartan is a medium pocket knife that is intended to fulfil a wide range of uses. It is available in many different graphical forms as well as with either blackened or polished stainless tools; it features 12 functions.

Key Features
Item number: 0.3603
1. Large blade
2. Small blade
3. Corkscrew
4. Can opener
5. Small screwdriver
6. Bottle opener
7. Screwdriver
8. Wire stripper
9. Punch reamer
10. Key ring
11. Tweezers
12. Toothpick

Dimensions
Height 0.6in
Length 3.3in
Weight 1.8oz

Cyber Tool L

The Cyber Tool L is a medium pocket knife that is intended for use by people who want to be able to work on IT gadgets at short notice. It has 39 functions including a variety of different screwdriver bits— Phillips, Torx and flat—as well as many of the more conventional tools.

Key Features
Item number 1.7775.T
1. Large blade
2. Small blade
3. Corkscrew
4. Can opener
5. Small screwdriver
6. Bottle opener
7. Screwdriver
8. Wire stripper
9. Punch reamer
10. Key ring
11. Tweezers
12. Toothpick
13. Bit wrench
14. Female Hex drive 5mm for D-SUB connectors
15. Female Hex drive 4mm for the bits
16. Bit Phillips 0
17. Bit Phillips 1
18. Bit case
19. Bit slotted 4
20. Bit Phillips 2
21. Bit Hex 4
22. Bit Torx 8
23. Bit Torx 10
24. Bit Torx 15
25. Pressurized ballpoint pen
26. Stainless steel pin
27. Mini screwdriver
28. Pliers
29. Wire cutters
30. Wire crimping tool
31. Scissors
32. Multipurpose hook
33. Wood saw
34. Nail file
35. Metal file
36. Nail cleaner
37. Metal saw
38. Fine screwdriver
39. Chisel

Dimensions
Height 1.3in
Length 3.6in
Weight 6.6oz

Traveller Lite

The Traveller Lite is a medium pocket knife that features 30 different functions, including an LED flashlight. Several of these have been brought in from other models to make a really useful tool that incorporates things like a barometer and thermometer. These useful extra functions are housed in the elegant handle where the Victorinox emblem doubles  as a button for selecting the electronic functions. The display can be illuminated to make the features easier to use. 3V lithium batteries provide the power required for the LED and the electronic functions. This multi-tool also contains an extra-strong Phillips screwdriver and a range of other useful tools in a very compact design.

Key Features

Item number 1.7905.AVT

1. Large blade
2. Small blade
3. Corkscrew
4. Can opener
5. Small screwdriver
6. Bottle opener
7. Screwdriver
8. Wire stripper
9. Punch reamer
10. Key ring
11. Tweezers
12. Toothpick
13. Scissors
14. Multipurpose hook
15. Nail file
16. Pressurized ballpoint pen
17. Stainless steel pin
18. Mini screwdriver
19. Digital watch (12h) or
20. Digital watch (24h)
21. Alarm
22. Countdown
23. Timer
24. Altimeter (m)
25. Altimeter (feet)
26. Barometer
27. Thermometer (°C)
28. Thermometer (°F)
29. Phillips screwdriver
30. LED

Dimensions

Height 1in
Length 3.6in
Weight 3.9oz

Swiss Champ XAVT

Key Features

Item number 1.6795.

XAVT

1. Large blade
2. Small blade
3. Corkscrew
4. Can opener
5. Small screwdriver
6. Bottle opener
7. Screwdriver
8. Wire stripper
9. Punch reamer
10. Key ring
11. Tweezers
12. Toothpick
13. Scissors
14. Multipurpose hook
15. Wood saw
16. Fish scaler
17. Hook disgorger
18. Ruler (cm)
19. Ruler (inches)
20. Nail file with
21. Metal file
22. Nail cleaner
23. Metal saw
24. Fine screwdriver
25. Chisel
26. Pliers
27. Wire cutters
28. Wire crimping tool
29. Phillips screwdriver
30. Magnifying glass

31. Pressurized ballpoint pen
32. Stainless steel pin
33. Mini screwdriver
34. Pharmaceutical spatula
35. Pruning blade
36. Electrician's blade
37. Wire scraper
38. Bit wrench
39. Female Hex drive 5mm for D-SUB connectors
40. Female Hex drive 4mm for the bits
41. Bit Torx 8
42. Bit Hex 4mm
43. Bit case with
44. Bit Phillips 0
45. Bit Phillips 1
46. Bit Phillips 2
47. Bit slotted 4mm
48. Bit Torx 10
49. Bit Torx 15
50. Bit wrench
51. Female Hex drive 5mm for D-SUB connectors
52. Female Hex drive 4mm for the bits
53. Bit Hex 2
54. Bit Hex 2.5
55. Bit case with
56. Bit Torx 6

57. Bit Torx 8
58. Bit slotted 3 x 1
59. Bit slotted 4 x 1
60. Bit Hex 1.2
61. Bit Hex 1.5
62. Large blade with wavy edge
63. LED
64. Universal wrench M2.5, M3, M4, M5
65. Multipurpose hook
66. Nail file
67. Punch reamer combination tool
68. Bottle opener
69. Can opener
70. Screwdriver
71. Wire stripper
72. Watch opener
73. Fine screwdriver
74. Digital watch (12h)
75. Digital watch (24h)
76. Alarm
77. Countdown
78. Timer
79. Altimeter (m)
80. Altimeter (feet)
81. Barometer
82. Thermometer (°C)
83. Thermometer (°F)

Dimensions

Height 2.6in

Length 3.6in

Weight 12.4oz

The Swiss Champ XAVT is the biggest collector's item for good reason
—with 83 functions, it has more than any other Swiss Army Knife ever
produced. Made up of 118 parts, weighing in at 350 grams (12.4oz),
and measuring 65mm wide, versatility of use and quality are the key
factors. Every Swiss Champ XAVT is manufactured in more than 500
meticulous steps and adeptly assembled by hand.

Huntsman Lite

The Huntsman Lite is a medium pocket knife designed to be used by anyone who ventures away from the beaten path and wants to be equipped to deal with any eventuality they may face. Using as little space as possible, it features a wood saw, an LED flashlight, a mini screwdriver, a strong Phillips screwdriver, a stainless steel pin, a ballpoint pen, and scissors, as part of its 21-function array of tools.

Key Features
Item number 1.7915.T
1. Large blade
2. Small blade
3. Corkscrew
4. Can opener
5. Small screwdriver
6. Bottle opener
7. Screwdriver
8. Wire stripper
9. Punch reamer
10. Key ring
11. Tweezers
12. Toothpick
13. Scissors
14. Multipurpose hook
15. Wood saw
16. Fine screwdriver
17. Pressurized ballpoint pen
18. Stainless steel pin
19. Mini screwdriver
20. Phillips screwdriver
21. LED

Dimensions
Height 1in
Length 3.6in
Weight 4.3oz

Spartan Lite

The Spartan Lite is a medium pocket knife that is stripped back to provide a combination of function and light weight. Where the Huntsman Lite weighs 4.3oz, this model only tips the scales at 2.9oz, however, it still provides 15 different functions, including a white LED flashlight.

Key Features
Item number 1.7804.T
1. Large blade
2. Small blade
3. Corkscrew
4. Can opener
5. Small screwdriver
6. Bottle opener
7. Screwdriver
8. Wire stripper
9. Punch reamer
10. Key ring
11. Tweezers
12. Toothpick
13. Phillips screwdriver
14. Mini screwdriver
15. LED flashlight

Dimensions
Height 0.8in
Length 3.6in
Weight 2.9oz

Large Pocket Knives

The models which are categorized as "Large Pocket Knives" all feature a locking mechanism for the main blade—this is to ensure complete safety and confidence when in use. Designed with a particular emphasis on this as well as functionality and robustness, many of them are aimed at specific markets, such as the "Skipper" model for sailors, the "Hunter" for the outdoor enthusiast, and the "Rescue Tool" for those who might end up in emergency situations. They all feature a heavy duty riveted construction and have robust ergonomically designed scales to provide a firm hold.

Sentinel	Ranger Grip 55	Ranger Grip 58 Hunter
Picknicker	Ranger Wood 55	Ranger Grip 71 Gardener
Alpineer	Ranger Grip 79	Ranger Grip 74
Forester Wood	Ranger Grip 179	Ranger Grip 174 Handyman
Forester	Ranger Grip 57	Ranger Grip Boatsman
Adventurer	Ranger Grip 53	Hunter Pro
Trailmaster	Ranger Grip 78	
Swiss Soldier's Knife 08	Ranger Grip 178	
Locksmith		
Outrider		
Hercules		
Work Champ		
Work Champ XL		
Cheese Knife		
Hunter		
Hunter XS Grip		
Hunter XT Grip		
Equestrian		
Rescue Tool		
Skipper		
Ranger Grip 52		
Ranger Grip 63		
Ranger Grip 61		
Ranger Grip 68		

Work Champ XL

The Work Champ XL is a large pocket knife that was designed as a portable tool chest. It has 30 functions including combination pliers, metal saw and file, wire stripper and wood saw, corkscrew, Phillips screwdriver and can opener. A robust model, it is ruggedly built and in Victorinox's words, "ready for anything—there's no obstacle the Work Champ XL can't tackle."

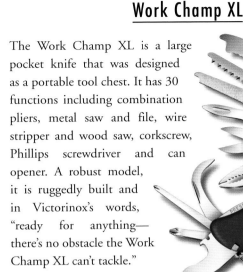

Key Features
Item number 0.8564.XL
1. Large blade
2. Bottle opener
3. Lockable screwdriver 5mm
4. Wire stripper
5. Wood saw
6. Metal saw
7. Metal file
8. Screwdriver 5mm
9. Wire stripper
10. Bottle opener
11. Can opener
12. Hoof cleaner
13. Can opener
14. Screwdriver 3mm
15. Seatbelt cutter
16. Shackle opener
17. Marlin spike
18. Punch reamer
19. Phillips screwdriver 0/1, long
20. Scissors
21. Phillips screwdriver 1/2
22. Pliers
23. Wire cutter
24. Wire crimping tool
25. Gutting blade
26. Tweezers
27. Toothpick
28. Key ring
29. Mini screwdriver
30. Corkscrew

Dimensions
Height 1.6in
Length 4.4in
Weight 12oz
Scale material Polyamide
Lockable blade Yes
One-hand blade Yes

Hunter

The Hunter is a large pocket knife that was specially designed to accompany hunters and serious outdoor enthusiasts into the wilderness. It has twelve functions including a large blade with a curved shape and a rounded tip for gutting game in the field, as well as most of the other tools one would expect on a knife like this.

Key Features
Item number 0.8573
1. Large blade
2. Screwdriver 5mm
3. Wire stripper
4. Bottle opener
5. Can opener
6. Small gutting blade
7. Punch reamer
8. Corkscrew
9. Wood saw
10. Tweezers
11. Toothpick
12. Key ring

Dimensions
Height 0.7in
Length 4.4in
Weight 4.4oz
Scale material Polyamide
Lockable blade Yes
One-hand blade No

Wine Master

The Wine Master is, as the name would suggest, a pocket knife for wine connoisseurs—be they professional sommeliers or amateur gourmets. It features an extra-long corkscrew with five coils to prevent cork breakage, plus a unique combination tool houses a two-step lever for uncorking alongside a bottle opener. Its viticultural credentials are intended to do your fine wine the honor it deserves. The integrated pocket knife has a wavy-edged beak blade foil cutter and a large locking blade, ideal for cheese or your favorite culinary tidbits.

Key Features
Item number 0.9701.63
Collection Wood
Two-step lever for uncorking wine bottles
Including leather pouch
1. Large blade
2. Corkscrew
3. Foil cutter
4. Two step lever
5. Bottle opener
6. Key ring

Dimensions
Height 0.7in
Length 5.1in
Weight 4.1oz
Scale material Walnut wood
Lockable blade Yes
One-hand blade No

Swiss Soldier's Knife 08

The Swiss Soldier's Knife 08 was designed to build on the knowledge gained over the last 100 years since the Swiss Army Officer's Knife was first produced. It is billed as the essential companion for outdoor enthusiasts, having ten functions and two-component scales for an outstanding grip as well as a large lock blade for one hand with 2/3 wavy edge.

Key Features
Item number 0.8461.MWCH
1. Large blade with wavy edge
2. Punch reamer
3. Bottle opener
4. Locable screwdriver 5mm
5. Wire stripper
6. Wood saw
7. Phillips screwdriver 1/2
8. Can opener
9. Screwdriver 3mm
10. Key ring

Dimensions
Height 0.7in
Length 4.4in
Weight 4.6oz
Scale material Two-component
   scales
Lockable blade Yes
One-hand blade Yes

Skipper

The Skipper is a large pocket knife designed for use in sailing. It combines typical Victorinox functionality with sailing-specific tools like a shackle opener and a marlin spike as well as other functions that are useful in a marine environment, such as a wire crimping tool and pliers. It comes equipped with a lanyard so that it always at hand when needed.

Key Features

Item number 0.8593.2W
1. Lanyard
2. Large blade with wavy edge
3. Bottle opener
4. Lockable screwdriver 5mm
5. Wire stripper
6. Shackle opener
7. Marlin spike
8. Can opener
9. Screwdriver 3mm
10. Punch reamer
11. Corkscrew
12. Phillips screwdriver 1/2

13. Pliers
14. Wire cutter
15. Wire crimping tool
16. Tweezers
17. Toothpick
18. Key ring

Dimensions

Height 0.9in
Length 4.4in
Weight 6.5oz
Scale material Polyamide
Lockable blade Yes
One-hand blade No

RescueTool

The RescueTool was developed and perfected in cooperation with emergency medical and rescue services in a five-year project. The key functions can be opened in seconds and are ready for use immediately. The rounded belt cutter can be used to cut through seatbelts. As the window breaker and disc saw tools are subject to particular wear and tear when used, they are easy to replace. All tools that have to be available quickly can be opened wearing gloves and are suitable for both right- and left-handed users. The one-handed blade and strong screwdriver (crate opener) are fixed in position when open with a liner lock mechanism. Even the look, with its luminescent yellow grip shells, is something special. It is also supplied with a bright red/yellow nylon case and a wide belt loop that fits a range of special-purpose belts.

Key Features
Item number 0.8623.MWN
In nylon pouch
Luminescent scales
1. Lock blade
   with 2/3 wavy edge
2. Phillips screwdriver
3. Window breaker
4. Lockable bottle opener
5. Screwdriver/crate opener
6. Wire stripper
7. Punch reamer
8. Seatbelt cutter

9. Key ring
10. Tweezers
11. Toothpick
12. Disk saw for shatterproof glass
13. Lanyard

Dimensions
Height 0.8in
Length 4.4in
Weight 5.9oz
Scale material Polyamide
Lockable blade Yes
One-hand blade Yes

Ranger Grip 71 Gardener

The Ranger Grip 71 is a large pocket knife which incorporate a pair of heavy-duty scissors that can be used for pruning plants. It also comes equipped with a wood saw, a large lock blade, and two-component scales that ensure excellent grip at all times. Like all of the knives in the Ranger series, it's made for skilled craftsmen and professionals.

Key Features
Item number 0.9713.C
1. Lock blade
2. Wood saw
3. Heavy-duty scissors with lever
4. Corkscrew
5. Key ring
6. Tweezers
7. Toothpick

Dimensions
Height 1.1in
Length 5.1in
Weight 7.7oz
Scale material Two-component scales
Lockable blade Yes
One-hand blade No

SwissTools

This range of multi-tools is built on two basic formats—the Swiss Tool, and the slightly smaller Swiss Tool Spirit. Their primary aim is to provide a robust platform which can deliver precision, versatility and stability whenever it is needed. They feature strong, ergonomically designed handles made of finely polished, easy-care stainless steel, and every tool is accessible from the outside for ultimate convenience. Each one is retained in place with its own spring and lock and as Victorinox themselves state "It's the ultimate expression of the Swiss Army Knife DNA."

Swiss Tool Spirit X 3.0224.L
Swiss Tool Spirit XC 3.0227.L
Swiss Tool Spirit XC Plus 3.0238.L
Swiss Tool Spirit XC Plus Ratchet 3.0239.L
Swiss Tool 3.0323.L
Swiss Tool X 3.0327.L
Swiss Tool X Plus 3.0338.L
Swiss Tool X Plus Ratchet 3.0339.L

131

Sport Tools

There are two basic Sport Tools—the Golf Tool and the Bike Tool, as well as several sturdy outdoor knives in this range. The first two were specifically designed by passionate practitioners to provide all the functionality that someone involved in either sport could require, and come in intelligently packaged arrangements that minimize their presence until needed.

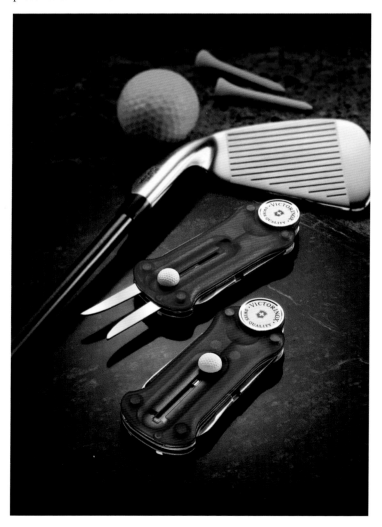

Golf Tool

Key Features
Item number
0.7052.T
1. Large blade
2. Tee punch
3. Bottle opener
4. Nail file
5. Groove cleaner
6. Scissors
7. Repair tool
8. Toothpick
9. Tweezers
10. Ballmarker

Dimensions
Height 0.6in
Length 3.6in
Weight 2.3oz
Scale material Polyamide
Size 4in
Lockable blade No
One-hand blade No

Available in black and red or blue translucent, this handy sporting tool boasts ten functions for the keen golfer. With its repair tool, ball marker, tee punch, groove cleaner, cap lifter, nail file, blade, tweezers, toothpick, and scissors, this essential quality tool is a must have for the golfing enthusiast. The tee punch is intended to help you tee up, even on hard or frozen ground, while the repair tool is there to assist with repairing the green. Likewise, the ball marker can be slid out as needed.

BikeTool

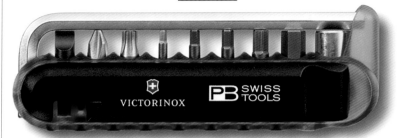

The BikeTool was designed by passionate enthusiasts as a Sport Tool with 12 functions for keen cyclists. At just 98 grams in weight and packaged very efficiently, it is both light and unobtrusive enough to be carried at all times. It is intended to help you keep your machine in tip-top condition through the provision of a tire lifter and a wide range of driver bits.

Key Features
Item number
4.1329
1. Bit case
2. Bit wrench
3. Hex 5
4. Adapter
   magnetic
5. Bit slotted 3
6. Bit Phillips 2
7. Bit Torx 25
8. Bit Hex 2
9. Bit Hex 2.5
10. Bit Hex 3
11. Bit Hex 4
12. Bit Hex 6
13. Tire lifter

Dimensions
Height 1.4in
Length 3.9in
Weight 3.2oz

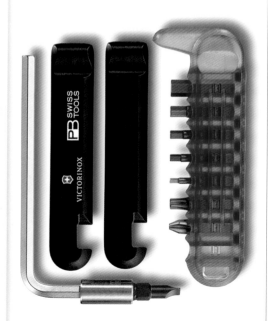

Barbeque Fork

While the Lightweight and Extendable Barbecue Fork is not strictly a Swiss Army Knife, it is certainly a perfect complement to them! How better to celebrate summer than through a barbecue with family and friends? A savory smell in the air, great surroundings, and a relaxed atmosphere. With this in mind, Victorinox designed the Barbecue Fork. Lightweight and easily extendable, it's the perfect tool to let nothing come between you and your food.

Key Features
Item number 4.2460
Lightweight
Stainless steel

Dimensions
Height 1.3in
Length closed 5.8in
Length extended 25.75in
Weight 2.7oz

Outdoor Knives

The Muela Outdoor Knives are billed as "The Outdoor Tool for Primitive Living"—as such, they are considered "wilderness-ready," and have been developed to deal with everything from bone to hard wood while being used for such tasks as carving, cutting, splitting, scraping, boring, hide tanning, and game dressing.

Muela Scout Knife

Key Features
Stainless steel, blade length 4.75in, in leather sheath

Muela Hunting Knife

Key Features
4.2243 Stainless steel, blade length 6.3in, in plastic sheath
4.2244 Stainless steel, blade length 6.3in, in leather sheath

SOS Outdoor Knife

Although it is manufactured and distributed by Victorinox, the SOS Outdoor knife was designed by Christof Hagen who runs the Survival Outdoor School (SOS). It has handles made of warm olive wood and a robust riveted-construction leather sheath.

With a blade length of 4.75in, it was designed to do everything you need to do outdoors including creating fire, building a shelter, outdoor cooking, game processing, and wood working (carving wood to create useful items from raw wood). The blade has a 20-degree hollow grind, delivering a sharp edge out of the box and is made from a INOX-1-42-MOVA, a type of high quality stainless steel.

Key Features
Type Fixed Blade
Class Outdoor
Blade Length 4.75in
Blade Design Drop Point
Blade Steel INOX-1-42-MOVA
Edge 20 degrees
Blade Thickness 0.13in
Total Length 9.7in
Handle material—Olive wood
  with finger grooves
Handle Color—Warm wood
Sheath—Tan leather

SwissCards

The SwissCard is a superb award-winning design concept—a whole variety of useful tools housed in a package that has the same length and width as a credit card. There are three basic formats: the SwissCard, the SwissCard Lite, and the SwissCard Nailcare, all of which fit into the slots in regular wallets, making them supremely practical for everyday use. There are also several different dedicated pouches on offer so that they can be carried in pockets and bags—these come in either real or imitation leather.

Swiss Card Classic

Key Features

Item number 0.7100.T

1. Letter opener (blade)
2. Scissors
3. Tweezers
4. Toothpick
5. Pressurized ballpoint pen
6. Stainless steel pin
7. Ruler (cm)
8. Ruler (inches)
9. Nail file
10. Screwdriver

Dimensions

Height 0.2in

Length 3.2in

Weight 0.9oz

The SwissCard Classic, which comes with ten functions all neatly packed into an area the size of a credit card. Combining clever, award-winning design, and incredible functionality, it is an extremely efficient way of carrying a wide variety of useful tools in an unobtrusive way.

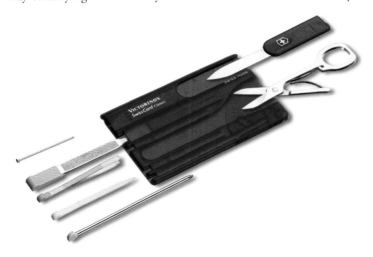

SwissCard Lite

The SwissCard Lite comes in the standard credit card format and boasts an integrated light diode as well as a precise magnifying glass and Victorinox's very own specially developed "Quattro" screwdriver with four functions. Elegant and compact, the SwissCard Lite fits easily into a diary, planner, purse, briefcase, or bag. Weighing just 20g, its dimensions are 3.2in long by 2.1in wide and is just 3.5mm in depth. A red light diode guarantees minimum energy which is supplied by a 3V lithium battery (which only needs changing after two years or intensive use) built neatly into the casing. It has 13 different functions, including a letter opener (blade); scissors; magnifying glass; pin; press ballpoint pen; 3mm and 5mm "Quattro" screwdrivers; a light diode; a ruler (in centimetres and inches); as well as the Phillips screwdriver (00-0 and1-2). This is a first-rate practical all-round product of the highest quality which was awarded the Design Prize at the Frankfurt Expo with its transparent color enabling the user to pick the correct tool easily.

Key Features

Item number 0.7300.T

1. Letter opener (blade)
2. Scissors
3. Tweezers
4. Pressurized ballpoint pen
5. Stainless steel pin
6. Ruler (cm)
7. Ruler (inches)
8. Magnifying glass
9. Screwdriver 3mm
10. Screwdriver 5mm
11. Phillips screwdriver 00—0
12. Phillips screwdriver 1—2
13. LED flashlight

Dimensions

Height 0.2in
Length 3.2in
Weight 0.9oz

Garden

The knives that Victorinox make for the horticultural industry have been renowned for decades for being incredibly sharp—this minimizes damage to the plants concerned and makes it a pleasure to use them. Intended for assisting with growing, grafting, and looking after fruit trees and ornamental plants, there are four basic formats—the Pruning Knife, the Floral Knife, the Flower and Grape Gatherer, and the Budding Knife. Within this family there are many variants, providing plenty of choice for the user.

CHAPTER 9

COLLECTING SWISS ARMY KNIVES

There are many collectors of pocket knives, particularly in the USA, where the finest handmade folding knives can change hands for thousands of dollars. There may be up to 5,000 brands and individual makers of folding knives for the collector to choose from, so most people will specialize in collecting one particular brand, type or era of knife. If you are not going to go for knives individually made by craftsmen, then the Swiss Army Knife could be the best alternative choice. Both the makers of these knives have concentrated from the start on building and maintaining a reputation for very high quality products and for using the finest materials available at any time. Victorinox, even today, boasts that 90 people, 10% of the workforce, are employed in checking that every knife is free from defects in material or workmanship. Many of the knife models are still assembled by hand; the bestselling lines are produced in such large quantities that automation is essential for these. Two major museums, in Germany and in New York, have also added the knives to their collections as examples of the finest 20th century design.

SCHLACHT BEI
BATTLE OF MURTEN 1476

SAMMLERMESSER - COLLECTOR'S KNIFE
EDITION 1989
BY VICTORINOX OF SWITZERLAND

The 1989 Collector's Knife commemorated the defeat of Charles the Bold of Burgundy in the 1476 Battle of Murten.

Specialist Collections

There are really no rules when it comes to deciding which type of knife you are going to collect. Fashions change constantly and an item which is valued at hundreds of dollars today can become worthless if no other collectors are prepared to bid for it. The Swiss Army knife falls into a curious category for collectors. Both the Wenger and Victorinox knives have been factory-produced in their thousands throughout the 20th century, so there are a lot of knives out there. However, these are not impulse purchases or unwanted gifts which lie unused in a drawer for years, nor are they ornaments, lovingly dusted and displayed. The owner of a well-designed, efficient pocket knife will find a hundred uses for it every day and will probably not part with it until the blades and springs are beyond repair, which, in the case of the Swiss Army Knife, can be a very long time.

It is sometimes possible to pick up a knife in good condition at a second hand or in junk stores, but do beware of imitations—always check that the maker's name or trademark is stamped on the base of the large blade. The Swiss emblem and characteristic red handles have been used by imitators all over the world and are no guide to the make of the knife.

Which Swiss Army Knife?

Collectors of Swiss Army Knives have first to decide whether they are going to go for both the brands which can truthfully bear that description; Victorinox and Wenger, or whether to choose just one brand. Elsener, now called Victorinox, were the first Swiss company to supply their knives to the Swiss army, so they can legitimately call their products the "original" Swiss Army Knives. However, the company which later became known as Wenger S.A. started supplying the army ten years after Elsener and have shared the contract since 1893—so the distinction is a fine one.

Neither company has retained the same brand name throughout their history. Wenger started as Paul Boechat & Cie, based in Courtételle in the Delémont valley in Switzerland's Jura region. In 1895 a group of entrepreneurs bought out Boechat and built a new cutlery manufacturing plant in Courtételle. In 1897 Theodore Wenger was hired as general manager and expanded production to include spoons and forks as well as pocket and table knives. In 1900 a new plant was opened, now called Fabrique Suisse de Coutellerie et Services. By 1908 Wenger had bought the company and renamed it Wenger & Cie.

Victorinox has gone through many changes of name in its history, although the company has stayed in the same location, Ibach in the canton of Schwyz, and is still owned by the founder's family. From 1884 Karl Elsener traded as an individual master cutler with the trade mark Elsener-Schwyz. In 1909, on the death of his mother, Elsener chose her first name, Victoria, as the firm's trademark. Following the introduction of the first stainless steel knives in 1923 the word "Inoxyd" was added to the trademark (from *inoxydable*, French for stainless) and by 1931 the two words had been combined to form the current company name of Victorinox. The trademarks Victoria and Elinox were also used for other cutlery produced by the company up until 1957.

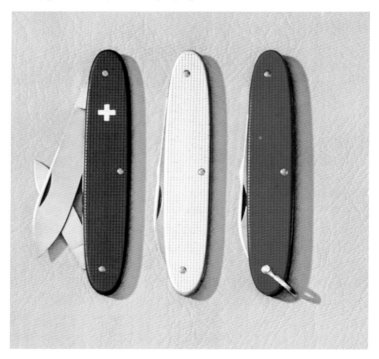

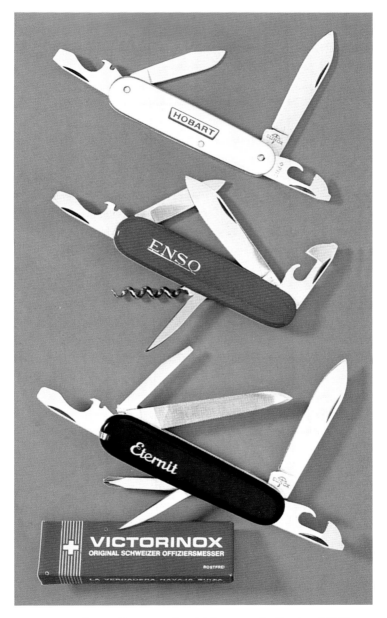

LEFT: A page from a Victorinox Spanish language leaflet dated 1958.

ABOVE: An "Ecoline Knife" from a 1965 leaflet.

LEFT: A page from the 1942 catalog showing sample promotional knives such as Omega watches.

ABOVE: These knives are taken from a 1951 catalog and show "strong pocket knives for country people."

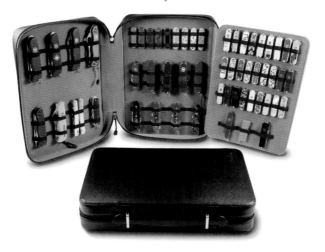

Collecting Today's Knives

Back to the Future must be a favorite movie for all collectors. The idea of being able to travel back in time and buy that desirable first edition, still in mint condition in its proper presentation case, and with the relevant trade catalog, and descriptive leaflet is a beguiling one. So far, though, the only way we can travel in time is forward, so many collectors are laying down stocks of future collectibles as they come out of the factory. With so many models to choose from, this could prove to be an expensive hobby, but it is possible to be selective and to choose those items which are likely either to become the classics of the future, or to highlight a particular facet of our age.

One of the original SwissCards, kept with its leather presentation pouch, may in 50 years time be prized as the first in a long line of

Leather Collectors and Presentation Briefcase
Item number 9.6954.0
Height 260mm
Length 360mm
Weight 1.5kg
This elegant Victorinox briefcase is designed to fit every model of Swiss Army Knife, so it's a great way to present your collector's items and to take your indispensable tools with you when you travel.

The White House has been an enthusiastic supporter of the Swiss Army
Knife; here are three of the special presidential editions of the Classic.

ever more sophisticated multi-tool cards. Or it may conjure images of
a time when those sweet old fashioned business people used to carry
strange oblong plastic cards around with them. Special editions of
the Victorinox knife are produced to cater for the particular needs of
sporting trends, some of which may endure, while some disappear into
the history books. There are Bike Tool Kits, Mountain Bike Tool Kits,
Golfer's knives (complete with divot fixer), and special kits for Inline-
Skaters. The Timer knife, with a conventional Swiss watch built in to

the handle may become a curiosity in a future age when only digital chronometers exist. New specials are always being developed, so the modern collector will have plenty to choose from.

An advantage of this type of collection is that the collector can verify the origin of the knife and be sure that it is not a fake. Keep any leaflets that come with the knife and, if possible, the trade and consumer catalogues which promote the introduction of a new line. A white SwissCard was issued in 1999, with a special "Mother's Day" presentation pack. A complete pack of this kind would be of much greater curiosity value in years to come than a SwissCard alone. Even copies of magazine advertisements or reviews from the "gadgets" columns of newspapers can make an interesting package and add to the future value of your collection.

Commemorative Knives and Special Editions

Perhaps the most obvious and, in some ways, the easiest form of collecting is to seek out knives which commemorate events and anniversaries. These knives are much more likely to be found in mint condition, even in their presentation cases, as they may have been bought not just as tools but as gifts or specifically for collections. The Love Ride is a charity event run on Harley Davidsons which has raised millions of dollars for the benefit of a variety of organisations, such as the Muscular Dystrophy Association. Victorinox have been enthusiastic supporters as pictured here (opposite and overleaf).

A number of special presentation kits have been produced to commemorate the anniversaries of the companies producing the knives, for example Victorinox produced a special edition of both the Classic and the SwissChamp, with engraved presentation case and leaflet, in 1997 for the centenary of the company. Each Centenary knife was numbered, with the numbers engraved on the divider behind the corkscrew. Although many thousands were produced, they would still be worth considerably more to the collectors of the future than an ordinary knife. During the years 1983–1991 Victorinox produced

Victorinox has supported the Love Ride with Harley Davidson and KTM.

ABOVE: The "Swiss Blade Harley" seen at the Love Ride.

BELOW: The Victorinox KTM Super Duke built by Motor-Center Schwyz.

seven Collector's knives commemorating famous battles of the Swiss defending the freedom of their country. A leaflet describing the battles and historical context was presented with the knives.

The Classic Limited Edition 2017 is a small pocket knife with animal graphics. 2017 marked the sixth anniversary of the Victorinox Classic Limited Edition Design Contest, and it came with an exciting twist. The creative competitors were given the theme "Animals of the World," a brief that was met with 1,254 design submissions from all over the world. The resulting versatile collection comes from Switzerland, Germany, Romania, Mexico, Denmark, Australia, and the US. From the feathers of the vividly colored parrot, to honey bees whose comb is the knife's scales, to a woodworm creating patterning with its journey, to a dog walking in space, the ten chosen ideas sit together in a collection that's smart, whimsical, sweet and funny.

Key Features
Item number 0.6223.
L1710
Designs created and
chosen by customers
Collection Limited
Edition
1. Small blade
2. Scissors
3. Nail file
4. Screwdriver 2.5mm
5. Key ring
6. Toothpick
7. Tweezers

Dimensions
Height 0.35in
Length 2.28in
Weight 0.75oz

Key Features
High-grade Alox scales in orchid
2016 engraved on back
Item number 0.8201.L16
Collection Limited Edition
1. Large blade
2. Punch reamer
3. Can opener
4. Screwdriver 3mm

5. Bottle opener
6. Screwdriver 7.5mm
7. Wire stripper
8. Key ring

Dimensions
Height 0.5in
Length 3.7in
Weight 2.5oz

The Pioneer Alox Limited
Edition 2016 is a medium
pocket knife that was produced
in a purple orchid color. The Alox
scales were upgraded with a process
called Eloxal, which uses anodic
oxidation to create an extra
layer of protection against
damage and corrosion.
It was available
in three sizes,
but only in
2016.

The events commemorated with special knives do not always have to be momentous anniversaries. On their 1998 spring outing, Harley Davidson Club riders from Germany, Austria, and Switzerland visited the factory at Ibach. A Rider Fan Knife was presented to each of the riders on that occasion.

Classic with Presidential seal

Lyndon B. Johnson, as President of the United States, commissioned Victorinox to produce Classic knives bearing his signature, to be presented to guests at the White House. 4,000 visitors were given these knives in special presentation cases, but the tradition was followed by Presidents Reagan and Bush, and how many will now have a complete set of Presidents' knives? If you decide to start your collection with the latest designs, you still have some catching up to do; many promotional editions of the SwissCard were ordered, including a Bush Presidential Library Foundation edition, with seal and signature.

Classic with
Presidential seal.

At the lower end of the price range, there are Victorinox Classics in national colors and with the relevant flag on the scales. A complete set of these knives bought at a particular point in history could be fascinating in years to come, if national

On the occasion of the 100th anniversary of the Swiss Army Knife,
Victorinox played host to President George Bush and his wife Barbara.
Here they are seen assembling a knife in the workshops.

boundaries continue to change in the coming century as they have
done in our time.

On the occasion of the 100th anniversary of the Swiss Army Knife,
Victorinox played host to President George Bush and his wife Barbara.
Here they are seen assembling a knife in the workshops.

Not all of the modern Victorinox army knives bear the Swiss
emblem. Special editions have been produced for various armed forces
around the world. The German army were issued with a Swiss Army
Knife in olive green, marked with the German Eagle, with only the
maker's name on the blade shank to identify its origins. The Nigerian
Air Force ordered a large quantity with the addition of a curved blade
for cutting through knotted parachute lines in an emergency.

The American Space Administration NASA issued the standard
Master Craftsman design to its astronauts on the Space Shuttle
program. Although they are identical to the commercially available
knives, these bear the NASA stamp on the scales and would form a
prized part of any collection.

Individual commemorative and presentation knives may be
harder to find, but would be well worth adding to any collection.

NASA issues the Master Craftsman
design to astronauts in the Space
Shuttle program.

Distinguished visitors to the Victorinox factory over the years have
been presented with engraved knives. As an example when Hilary
Clinton visited Brunnen in the Swiss Knife Valley in 1998 she was
presented with a small Classic knife with hammered sterling silver
handles, engraved with the words "I am honored to give you this
token present commemorating your visit to the Swiss Knife Valley."
A commercial version of the silver-handled knife was introduced into
the range, but the original engraved knife will one day be a trophy in
someone's collection.

The turn of the millennium has brought a flood of commemorative items from manufacturers of every conceivable object. There may be brave collectors out there who will try to gather in every millennial product, but the sheer volume of goods available will mean that few gain in value for a very long time. It pays to stick to those articles which stand a chance of lasting, and the Victorinox Cyber Tool will surely be among the survivors.

Examples of Victorinox knives as promotional items.

Promotional Knives

The reputation of the Swiss Army Knife for quality and versatility has made it a useful symbol for companies wishing to attribute these qualities to their products. The chapter in this book on the use of the knives in other people's advertising attests to the appeal of the knives as a promotional gift.

Over the past 30 years many thousands of knives have been specially produced by Wenger and Victorinox for companies, from the tourist boards of Swiss cantons to chemical, engineering and automobile producers. Many of these knives bear the Swiss cross emblem in addition to the company's name on the scales, as the whole point of giving the knives as business gifts is to associate the company with a universally-known symbol of quality. Special presentation sets are also used as prizes and special awards in many companies today and may be engraved with the date and details of the award.

Collecting Knife Models

Since the first Soldier's knife and Officer's Knife, all the different models of Swiss Army Knives have been known by names rather than serial numbers. The names tend to reflect the uses to which the particular configuration of blades and tools is best suited, such as the Sportsman, the Executive, the Climber, Camper, and Huntsman. Some of the knives, such as Victorinox's Golfer and Fisherman, are engraved with an image suited to the name. As the range of knives available expanded, the companies have given them product identification numbers so that a particular configuration of implements can be identified, but these numbers do not appear on the knives and some detective work may be needed to identify the exact product and date of issue. Both companies have examples of product catalogues through the years and may be able to help in identifying a knife from its shape, weight, design of emblem, and maker's stamp on the blade and the tools and blades included in the knife. A collection which incorporates every style of blade and implement will have a greater curiosity value than a random selection of knives.

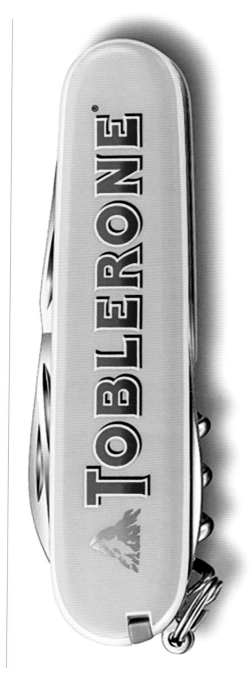

Bear in mind that not all Swiss Army Knives are red. Although this is the color which immediately comes to mind when people think of this type of knife, the modern Soldier's knife has silver-colored scales and variations on the standard designs have been produced over the years in camouflage patterns, national colors, natural horn, rosewood, black, blue, and a whole range of fashion colors.

Condition

If you are collecting modern Swiss Army knives, made within the

Not all Swiss Army Knives are red.

past 20 years, then you may be able to go for the ideal, which is to collect only knives in absolutely mint condition. They should be kept in their presentation boxes, unused and, above all, never sharpened, as this destroys the original finish on the blades. Cleaning and handling should be kept to an absolute minimum and the cases and handles kept out of direct, bright light to avoid fading.

Collectors of older knives, including the pre-stainless steel rust-prone type, may be tempted to improve the appearance of a new acquisition by mending cracks in the wooden handles, stripping off rust, or sharpening the blades. This destroys whatever value the knife may have had to the serious collector and may lead to suspicions that the knife has been reworked or made up from parts of other knives. When you are buying knives dating back to the early days of the Swiss Army Knife try to avoid those which have obviously been sharpened many times, or which have had springs replaced or handles mended.

A soft cloth may be used to wipe off surface marks and a small amount of machine oil or, if you can get it, Japanese sword oil, can help to ease the joints. Modern all-purpose oils such as 3-in-1 or WD-40 contain solvents and should never be used on any part of the knife. Active spots of rust can be scraped off using a needle and a little oil, but a future collector would much rather find rust stains on a blade than evidence of sandpaper. Ideally all knives, not just the rust-prone ones, should be kept in a damp-controlled environment. This is obviously not always possible, so the very basic rules of storage are that knives should never be stored for long periods of time inside leather cases—if a leather case comes with the knife then keep them separate. Acid-free paper can be obtained from picture framers (or may be advertised in knife magazines) for lining containers in which knives are to be kept. Check your collection regularly for signs of rust—immediate attention to a very small spot of active rust can save further deterioration.

If you decide to take up collecting, then information and contacts are available through the internet, knife magazines, and knife shows, where you will be able to find out about clubs and other collectors in your area. Victorinox have an international network of distributors and, in larger towns, there are usually retail outlets which carry the whole range of knives. It is worth finding the best shop in your area so

CHAPTER 10

A SYMBOL OF QUALITY
IN ADVERTISING

The manufacturers of most products would be astonished to see them used in advertisements for other companies' goods. Yet this happens all the time with the Swiss Army knife. In advertising they say that a picture is worth more than a thousand words. So, whenever advertisers seek to convey that their product is versatile, reliable, compact and of high quality, they have only to show the image of the Swiss Army Knife alongside their product. Consumers throughout the world understand instantly what it is they are trying to say and they can then concentrate in the text on the rest of their product's virtues. Victorinox already has a collection of more than 200 advertisements of important international companies.

The image has been used in print to sell everything from ice cream to photocopiers, either seriously, or subtly changed to convey a more humorous message. Advertisers selling financial products are particularly fond of the image, as it fulfils the dual role of assuring flexibility and cashing in on Switzerland's reputation as a safe banking haven.

The Victorinox knife has not quite managed to take over from the girl draped over the bonnet when it comes to selling cars. However, it does appeal to the "classier" end of the market for cars and motorbikes and has the advantage of being completely non-sexist.

You can drive it...

Service your truck with it...

Swiss Army Knives have become a symbol of utility and quality, and have become synonymous with versatility.

NOW YOU

CAN BE PREPARED

EVERY DAY.

Even sports writers use the image.

Raiders' new Swiss army knife

Once just a running back, Williams now does it all on offense

By Jim Jenkins
Bee Staff Writer

ALAMEDA – A major topic of conversation in training camp, the Raiders' Harvey Williams is now becoming a focal point of chitchat with opposing teams.

Williams has been converted from featured running back to multipurpose tight end, and defenses don't exactly know what to do with him.

The speedy but rugged 6-foot-2, 225-pounder rushed for 2,528 yards the last three seasons but now roams free in the Oakland offense.

Sometimes he lines up next to a tackle and blocks; sometimes he's deployed as a fullback for a running or blocking assignment; and often he's a receiver in motion, forcing linebackers and defensive backs to make last-second adjustments.

The New Orleans Saints were certainly confused during the Raiders' 18-16 preseason win Saturday, in which Williams caught a four-yard scoring pass from Jeff George. When he made the reception, five defenders were nearby, but none reacted fast enough to make a play.

Harvey Williams joins a long Raiders tradition of converting runners into all-purpose tight ends.

Associated Press photograph

Williams recalled when he was in one of his multiple sets, Saints linebacker Mark Fields asked him, "What are you doing over here?"

At first Williams did seem out of place in his new job. He had no choice in the move. During the offseason, new coach Joe Bugel decided he wanted Napo-

Please see RAIDERS, page D3

In the financial sector, you can buy
the Swiss Army Knife of mortgages, of
asset management, insurance, personal
banking, business banking, and credit
cards...

The knife that takes pictures...
and machines...

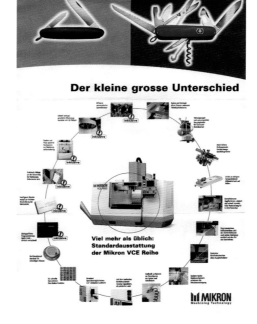

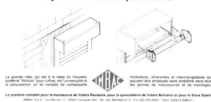

shuts your window blinds...
takes phone calls...

and tells the time.
This knife sells boats...

neat solutions

and credit.

It is the ultimate symbol for many high profile businesses...

and every computer in the world wants to be a Swiss Army Knife when it grows up.

)rder

Organisation is efficiency.
An efficient system gives you the right tools and is easily adapted to new demands.
Cashplan Plus streamlines the financial side of your business and will provide almost any type of information you require, instantly and to any level of detail. Day to day transactions and cashflow management are a breeze, and the powerful planning functions promote effective long term forecasting.
But unless the system fits into your way of doing things these features will be next to useless. That's where Cashplan Plus has a distinct advantage over others - it can be customised by it's users and *adapted for any number of tasks*. Your business will *never* outgrow Cashplan Plus.
Trying to explain all the features and how simple they are to run is beyond the scope of this brochure. The best way to find out more is to see for yourself. Because Cashplan Plus has been designed right here in New Zealand you can talk directly to the makers and call for a *FREE* demonstration.

Cashplan
PLUS

It's enough to make a computer jealous.

SATELLITE PRO 4200
ET MICROSOFT™ WINDOWS™ NT
WORKSTATION.
IL NE FAUT PAS DÉPENSER
DES FORTUNES POUR TOUT AVOIR.

179

CHAPTER 11

SEEING THE FUNNY SIDE

The Swiss Army Knife has been a boon to cartoonists and humorists. The very characteristics which give the knives their universal appeal can also seem slightly ridiculous and help us to laugh at ourselves. First we have the Swiss Army Bore, who has had his trusty knife since childhood and insists on taking it out and explaining each blade to anyone who will listen. This overgrown boy scout is always ready to step in and rescue us lesser mortals from our own oversights or stupidity with a tool tailor-made for the purpose. We love him really, but there is a part of us that wishes, just once, to see him in a situation where he does not have the tool for the job.

In the swinging sixties the Mini car started a fashion for miniaturisation which has never left us. Portable phones, laptop computers, and personal organizers vie to cram the maximum number of features into the smallest space possible. Cartoonists have had a great time exposing some of the wilder claims of the miniaturists, and the Swiss Army Knife provides the perfect vehicle for this. The Swiss Army Cat is a wonderful invention—it cuts, it chops, it shreds, and it never has to be sharpened. *National Lampoon* suggested a Swiss Army House, in which all the rooms neatly folded in to the blade so that it could be carried around. Let an illustrator loose on the Swiss Army concept and he can condense a whole lifestyle into a single red handle.

The age of the individualist has brought a need for us all to be completely self-sufficient in every situation and the pocket knife that does everything sums this up. The popular *MacGyver* television series took the concept of the pocket lifesaver to ridiculous extremes. Part of our affection for the Swiss Army Knife comes from a desire to be in control of technology. There are so many sophisticated electronic devises ruling our lives that the solid, old fashioned simplicity of the SAK comes as a blessed relief. Victorinox claim that the majority of the knives they sell are bought by women, mostly as presents for the men in their lives. If we take note of the cartoonists, it seems that there

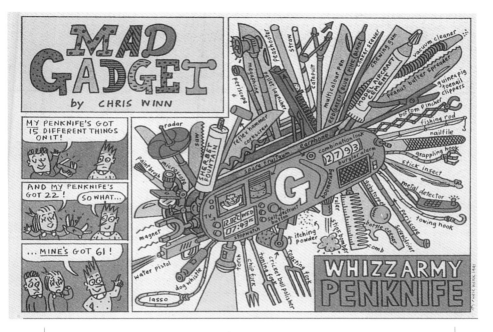

Chris Winn's homage to Victorinox.

is more to it than that. There may be a natural empathy between the Swiss Army Knife and today's working woman. The drawings of the Swiss Army Wife and the Swiss Army Mom sum up to perfection the range of functions they see themselves performing. Perhaps Victorinox should start producing a Soldier's Wife's knife.

CHAPTER 12

THE LEGEND OF THE
SWISS ARMY KNIFE

A Work of Art

The Victorinox Swiss Army Knife is a work of art, and that's official. In 1977 the Architecture and Design Department of the Museum of Modern Art in New York decided to include the Swiss Army Officer's Knife in their collection as an outstanding example of functional design. The State Museum of Fine Art in Munich, Germany have since also added the knife to their exhibition showing examples of the best in modern design. The model chosen was the Champion, forerunner of today's SwissChamp, but with only 24 features.

Of course the knives are not just displayed for their good looks—"fitness for purpose" is the benchmark of good design and in this chapter there are examples of the Swiss Army Knife's fitness both for its intended purpose and for purposes never dreamt of by its originators.

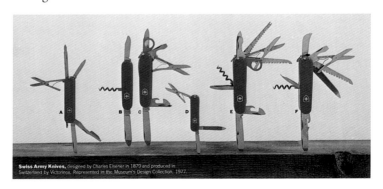

Swiss Army Knives, designed by Charles Elsener in 1879 and produced in Switzerland by Victorinox. Represented in the Museum's Design Collection, 1977.

Astro-Knives

Karl Elsener might have decided that it was time for a brisk walk in the hills around his home if he had woken from a dream of his Officer's Knife orbiting the earth, but his design has in fact proved very popular in space. As early as 1978 NASA, the American space organisation, ordered 50 Victorinox Master Craftsman Swiss Army Officer's Knives (Model no. 5044) for use by their astronauts. The knives were used extensively during the Skylab program and have been part of the very limited list of personal equipment carried by space shuttle astronauts since the first flight, along with sunglasses, surgical scissors, a watch, sleep-mask, and earplugs. The only modification to the commercially available design was the addition of a Velcro strip to stop the knife from flying out of the astronauts' pockets.

National Aeronautics and
Space Administration

NASA

Lyndon B. Johnson Space Center
Houston, Texas
77058

Reply to Attn of: AP3   November 15, 1978

Mr. John F. Zyla
Vice President
Sales and Marketing
Victorinox of Switzerland, Ltd.
49 Quail Court, Suite 304
Walnut Creek, California 94596

Dear Mr. Zyla:

Thank you for your letter of November 9, 1978, in which you request information on NASA's purchase of Victorinox Swiss Army Knives.

NASA has purchased 50 Victorinox Swiss Army Knives model #5044, Master Craftsman, through NASA's crew equipment contractor ILC Industries. These knives will be aboard the Space Shuttle Orbiter as part of crew equipment.

Although we are pleased to confirm the purchase of these knives, this confirmation must not be considered a commerical endorsement of your product by NASA.

We will be happy to work with you if Victorinox officials plan any news releases or advertisements of the fact that these knives will be part of the astronaut crew equipment.

Thank you for your letter and if we can be of additional help, please don't hesitate to contact this office.

Sincerely,

Robert Gordon
Manager of Industrial Communications
Office of Public Affairs

Space Shuttle

One of the first reports of the knife's use in a space emergency came in 1983, when Ulf Merbold, a German, became the first non-American to go into space on a space shuttle. A physicist from Stuttgart, Merbold was given a place on the shuttle in order to carry out 72 experiments in the custom-built laboratory at a height of 155 miles and a speed of 5 miles per second. During the first few days it became evident that, despite the millions of dollars spent and meticulous planning for the tasks to be carried out in space, there were teething troubles. As soon as Merbold went to open the first piece of equipment it emerged that he had been sent into space with the wrong kind of wrench. Imaginative use of his Swiss Army Knife solved this problem.

Shortly afterwards there was a failure in the reflector furnace in which an attempt was to be made to manufacture metal alloys under weightless conditions. Merbold's knife also had a screwdriver to fix the problem. It even turned out that a simple electrical plug had been incorrectly connected

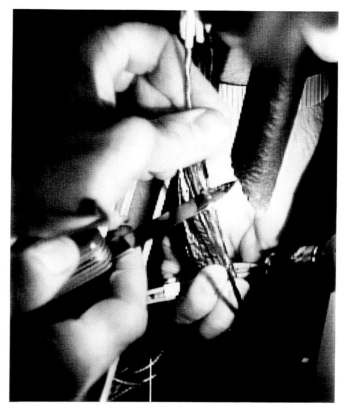

Ulf Merbold at work with his Swiss Army Knife.

to the base—again the Swiss Army Knife provided the tools for reconnection. Satellite TV viewers in the US and Europe watched every move and were delighted with the skill of this super space handyman. Even the Commander of the *Columbia* space shuttle, moon landing veteran John Young, was impressed with his passenger. "That guy over there" he said to Ground Control Station, "has really been slogging his guts out and he doesn't even have a good window seat." Merbold had rescued experiments costing countless millions with just a clear head and a Swiss Army Knife.

Discovery

In 1985, Victorinox received a letter from Edward M Payton, the brother of one of the astronauts on the space shuttle *Discovery*, asking where he could obtain a Master Craftsman.

"My brother needed this knife during his space flight to carry out a number of tasks. He was full of praise for this knife because it functioned so well even under the difficult conditions of space flight. After the flight he found that he also needed to use his Swiss knife virtually everyday here on Earth, on solid ground."

In May 1991, the space shuttle *Discovery* set off for another flight into near space. During the mission it was discovered that a piece of recording equipment was no longer functioning properly. The task of this piece of equipment was to record the data from two telescopes for scientific experiments. On the sixth day of the nine-day mission, Ground Control in Houston, Texas relayed their solution to the astronauts. New wires had to be connected to a complex computer. A very fine, sharp blade was needed to strip the insulation from the vital cables and the Swiss Army Knife proved the ideal tool. The computer was successfully reconnected and vital data rescued.

The Lifesaver

The Swiss Army regard these knives as part of a soldier's personal survival kit. In civilian life they have many times been responsible for ensuring the survival of victims of accidents and medical emergencies. These are just a few of the many anecdotes regularly sent to Ibach attesting to the lifesaving qualities of the knives.

Victorinox—My Third Hand

Pascal de Souza, technical director of an office that specializes in the study of parking facilities in cities, told us his story:

"It was late at night on December 30, 1999. It was raining as I drove along the minor road near to Paris that I had used hundreds of times before. It had been a demanding week. My alertness was blunted by Friday-evening tiredness, the to and fro of the windscreen wipers and the comforting knowledge that I was going home…then just one misjudged curve, sudden fright, like a bolt of lightning, and then the impact. My car had run off the road and landed in a ditch.

"In a few seconds I had come to my senses. I was trapped by my seat belt, which I could not unfasten. My car was stuck nose-down in a rainwater drainage ditch. The icy water was up to my waist and threatened to rise higher. Above, I could see the beams from the headlights of cars passing round the curve, but none of them could have spotted me … I had to depend on myself alone and in particular on my Victorinox. My pocket-knife, kept in its leather pouch on my belt, is never away from me. It is my faithful companion. It cut through the safety belt without difficulty, allowing me to struggle free of the car. Without the Victorinox I would certainly have been left stuck all night at the bottom of the ditch, and in that icy cold water I would have expected the worst …"

Pascal de Souza's story is just one example of how often life hangs on a single thread—in this case on the meticulously ground blade of a Swiss knife. Pascal goes so far as to say that the knife acted as his "third hand." And there would be some considerable truth in the claim. It has been part of his life for over 25 years. It is with him in both work and leisure.

Roadside Operation

The life of a nine-year-old boy hung by a thread in June 1990. Philip Byrne was spending his holidays with an aunt in County Meath, Ireland. He was hit by a car as he pedalled his bicycle along the road and suffered severe internal injuries. Purely by chance four Belfast surgeons were traveling in the car behind. They used a Swiss Army Knife to insert a drain in the boy's chest while waiting for the ambulance to arrive, saving Philip's life. The local media made much of the fact that such a procedure could be performed using just a pen knife, and of the boy's incredible luck in having his accident within sight of four of the best equipped surgeons in Ireland.

Amputations

More drastic surgery is possible using the SwissChamp's saw attachment, as shown by this letter dated September 1991 from Professor John Ross, a Canadian doctor training local doctors in rural Uganda.

"I started to work here two years ago. Part of my work is dedicated to the development of a hospital in a small town called Tororo, located close to the Kenyan border, some 300km away from Kampala, the capital of Uganda. I brought a wide range of surgical instruments with me, one of which was a good surgical saw for amputations. This type of instrument is needed here because there are many injuries, for example bullet wounds, which result in having to amputate an arm or leg. Shortly after my arrival here my surgical saw was stolen. So my Swiss Army Knife, which I always carry with me, was placed in boiling water to sterilize it. From then on I decided to use the saw on the knife for amputations.

"It worked very well. It actually took six months for me to get a new surgical saw. During this time I carried out at least six amputations using this knife saw. Although the knife lost its lovely red plastic cover due to being constantly boiled in water, the instrument otherwise worked faultlessly. The steel you use must be of excellent quality."

A Vet's Best Friend

Vets, as well, have made good use of the knives, practising as they do in many out-of-the-way places. Larry Anderson, a vet with a country practice in New Zealand, records that he has found hundreds of applications for his SwissChamp, including dental scaling, removing plasters, manicuring claws, and modifying surgical equipment for emergencies. He has even used the pliers, scissors, and tweezers for suturing a human head wound.

our team as well as our equipment was put to the test in a unique environment. Your Swiss Army Officer's Knives coped superbly well with their extensive use. It wasn't long before the knives became an indispensable tool for a range of tasks as well as in emergencies."

Frank Goodman was very sad when he lost his on Cape Horn Island. "I carried my knife in a life jacket pocket and as a result it frequently came into contact with salt water. Despite this, it continued to function perfectly. Many knives which are advertised as being 'stainless steel' rust precisely when they are needed most. These were obviously the genuine article."

North Pole Expedition

Another hazardous expedition proved the knives' ability to perform under extreme conditions, as Charles Burton reported following the British North Pole Expedition in the winter of 1976–1977.

"In July 1977 we returned to England after six months in the Arctic. The group of ice explorers spent 90 days on the pack ice at temperatures below 50° Celsius. This had been the lowest recorded temperature in the Arctic for 46 years. On May 15, despite having already covered 890 miles on the ice and just ten days away from the North Pole, we had to be evacuated. A break-up in the ice, something which had never happened before, forced us to return. Our Swiss Army Knives had proven invaluable for the entire group on the ice as well as for those at base camp. They were used amongst other things to remove ice from the sledge runners and for opening canned foods. When one of our party fell into the ice we

were able to use the knife to cut loose his clothing and free him from his wet garments, which immediately froze. When he fell into the ice the temperatures were -35°F, so he had to be taken into a tent quickly and dried out. Without this quick action with the help of your knives he could have been in serious danger."

Balloonists' World Height Record

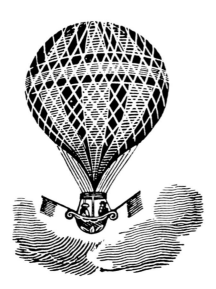

Recently many hot air ballooning records have been attempted, some more successfully than others. Victorinox have on file a report of the Swiss Army Knife's vital contribution to one of the earlier records, and we can be sure that pocket knives have been carried in the round the world ballooning race as well, given the limitations of space and the old maxim that if something can go wrong on a record attempt, then it will. In June 1988 the Swedish balloonist Lindstrand and entrepreneur Richard Branson attempted to break the world height record for hot air balloons. With preparations for the flight complete, they had to wait for more than a week to get a good start window because of high winds. Finally, at 5.42am on June 6, 1988 they set off in their pressurized aluminum capsule. Weather conditions were ideal; blue sky with a light wind. All seemed well, but they soon realized that, after all the nerve-wracking waiting, they had forgotten one small detail—two 100lb sacks of sand were still attached to the balloon. Lindstrand had to climb down from his capsule and cut these off using his pocket knife. The balloon then shot up to a new world record height of 11 miles.

MacGyver Escapes

Many of the stories about the miracle properties of the Swiss Army Knife emphasize the importance to the owners of having their knife with them at all times, not just when they are embarking on some hazardous outdoor exercise or adventure. Douglas MacIver, a 31-year old engineer living in Portland, Oregon, USA relates a tale of survival in a much more mundane setting than the adventurous knife may have been used to.

"I've carried a Victorinox Champ knife around with me for many years. It has proven its worth in no end of situations, but never more so than on the evening of December 3, 1992. On that evening my wife attended a Christmas Art-bizarre party. The party was hosted by the tenants of the Mattox Building, which houses various art studios for photographers, designers, architects, etc. I went to the fourth floor of the building, the top floor, where the party was being held, and stayed for about an hour. Needless to say after an hour I became bored and went looking for something more interesting. There are three ways to travel up and down the Mattox Building; a stairwell, a goods elevator, and a passenger elevator. This last was as old as the building itself which, I imagine, was mentioned somewhere in the last chapter of the *Bible*. The elevator was about three square feet in size and about 8ft high. The inner door consisted of a metal sliding grille, the outer one a very normal door. There was no telephone or escape hatch.

"As I was traveling in the elevator it suddenly began to slow down and fill with smoke. A few seconds later it came to an abrupt halt. I was alone and trapped. The elevator continued to fill with smoke. Because there wasn't much fresh air I had to breathe in the black, acrid smoke while the built-in loudspeaker constantly played a violin sonata in the background. The elevator had stopped on the mezzanine, just above the first floor. I was able to see approximately ten centimetres of the lift doors on the second floor and almost the whole of the doors on the mezzanine. People were gathered on the second floor. They started to talk to me through the lift doors. But we couldn't see each other.

Once they learned that the elevator had jammed and I was slowly but surely in danger of choking to death, they called the emergency control center.

"In the meantime, my friends noticed the smoke on the fourth floor. They quickly discovered that someone was stuck in the elevator and that a fire had broken out in the elevator shaft. Shortly afterwards they attempted to force open the doors on the second floor to release me. Then a whole contingent of the Portland Fire Department arrived. The greatest problem for my rescuers was that over the years the mezzanine had been sealed up. There was no way to reach the elevator doors on the mezzanine—my only escape route. Since no-one could reach me I did what I could to reach them. The mechanism responsible for opening the mezzanine doors had also been put out of action because this floor was no longer in use. Someone had removed the elevator door button which had been there for opening the doors. Otherwise I could have simply pressed the button to get out.

"But wait a minute; I had my trusty Swiss military knife with me and this had a pair of tweezers on it. Three minutes later I had removed the nuts on the door and was at last able to get out of the elevator. But now I was still trapped in the dead space of the mezzanine. In the meantime, the battalion of Fire Department people (four large fire appliances, two ambulances and two control vehicles) had put out the fire in the elevator shaft and were still trying to reach me. They had battered down doors to reach the floor of the shaft and climbed to the roof of the building to reach me from above. The police had cordoned off the entire block, which had since filled with curious onlookers.

"I could hear alarm bells ringing and sirens wailing. But there was a window on the mezzanine and that's where I was finally rescued from and where my martyrdom came to an end. But before then of course I had used my Swiss Army Knife once more to remove the hinges from the window. In the heat of the moment I left my valued Swiss Champ on the mezzanine. As the firemen accompanied me down the ladder, the crowd below applauded and I waved. Friends and reporters were waiting for me below. Luckily, a fireman found my knife and returned it to me. Next morning a radio station telephoned me and I was interviewed live. They had read the newspaper article about me and found it amusing to learn that not only had I fled from a jammed lift and escaped the fire with the help of my pocket knife, but that my name is MacIver, since MacGyver is the name of an American TV hero who repeatedly escapes from hopeless situations, most of the time with the help of a Swiss Army Knife.

"In the weeks that followed the Swiss Army Knife was one of the most popular Christmas gifts in Portland. I bought the last SwissChamp in a shop for a friend, noticing that the item was displayed in the shop front window. The shop owner told me that he had had a real run on SwissChamps following the incident. Another shopkeeper reported that every child who came into his shop wanted to buy a knife just like the 'lift escape knife.' "

A Lifeline in Your Pocket

Those who regard their pocket knife as an essential item of clothing can always rely on it to get them out of a tight spot. Helmut Knosp of Freiburg in Germany tells of a lucky escape from an air crash:

"On March 31, I crashed into the French Vosges on a flight from Reims to Freiburg in a four-seater sporting aircraft. My three flight comrades were killed on the spot. I escaped with a few broken bones in my arms and legs and other bruises and injuries. My life was saved thanks to a Swiss Army Officer's pocket knife. With the help of this knife I was able to free myself from the crumpled, burning machine by cutting through the jammed seat belt and then cutting my way through plastic trim and forcing my way out of the window. Since then I have named my pocket knife, my constant companion for many years 'Lifesaver' because if it hadn't been for its help, I would no longer be alive."

Atlantic Flight

Another air disaster was averted thanks to this most versatile of traveling tool kits, as related by an American admiral:

"I have carried my Victorinox friend with me since I started flying 23 years ago. One dark night in 1988, halfway across the Atlantic, I needed it to repair a broken oxygen mask. If I hadn't had the knife with me, I would have been left with no other choice but to fly much lower so I could breathe. However, this would have meant that the fuel would then not have been sufficient to reach the airport on the Azores (because of the increased air resistance). Or I would have had to remain flying at high altitude although this would have been very dangerous for me due to the risk of my passing out as a result of lack of oxygen. Neither of the two alternatives was a tenable option. Thanks to my super knife I was able to end my flight safely and as planned."

Capsized

John Townley, an American journalist, had his knife with him just at the moment when it was most needed:

"In 1991 I was crewing on a small sloop being delivered from the Chesapeake Bay to Mystic, Connecticut. After several days of problems breaking in the brand-new sailboat, we found ourselves in the often-treacherous waters 15 miles off Cape May, New Jersey, on a blustery afternoon, with scattered line squalls racing across the sky. The wind was brisk and the captain decided this was just the time and place to clap on all sail and 'see what she could do.' We hadn't been scudding merrily along more than 20 minutes under maximum sail when a squall hit us. In an instant, the boat was flat on its side, held prone against the swell by the tightened sail, whose lines were now frozen hard, up in the sheet blocks. As she began to take on water, we knew we had to right her quickly or we'd all go down to Davy Jones. The only way was to cut away the rigging and … we didn't have a single sailor's rigging knife on deck, between the four of us! Times like that,

the past begins to flash before your eyes ... Then I realized that I still had my Swiss Army knife in my pocket. In an instant it was out, and thanks to its still-keen edge, I began to cut away the sails, until at last the boat righted itself and we had time and stability to bail her out and start the auxiliary engine to make way against the storm. In just a few instants, my 'secondary' pocket tool had become the lifesaving instrument for four very wet and frightened sailors. Needless to say, I have never been without it since!"

The Portable Toolkit

Norwegian Tore Lund Bache was given a knife as a gift in 1968 by his company, OSO. In 1992 he wrote:

"The knife has been my companion for 25 years and has traveled with me all around the world. I always kept it in my left trouser pocket, even in my smoking jacket, ready for use at all times. The OSO company logo has almost completely disappeared. There are numerous stories involving this knife. It has become a legend among my friends. They always ask me the same question: 'Have you still got your OSO knife with you?'

"In 1969 I bought an old Willys Jeep, a Second World War model. It was a beautiful old vehicle and you could repair any of the parts (unlike today's vehicles on which broken parts have to be replaced). I immediately went for a spin into the desert to test the capabilities of the four-wheel drive. This test took me several kilometers into a marshy wooded area where no vehicle had obviously ever been before. And then my engine died. The problem was that the fuel supply was no longer getting to the engine—there was something wrong with the fuel pump. A quick look in my vehicle revealed that I didn't have any tools with me. All I had in my pocket was a little loose change, a ball-point pen, and my Victorinox knife. With the help of the knife I was able to scrape out and open the fuel pump. Although there were no screws on the pump I was able to use the bottle opener which fitted the lid exactly.

"The suction valve in the fuel pump had broken into several pieces. So I took my knife and fashioned a replacement part using the spring

on the ball pen. Although the knife hadn't actually saved my life on that occasion it nevertheless enabled me to repair my vehicle. This saved me having to walk several kilometers and probably the trouble of finding a tow-truck capable of towing my jeep back home. Today, after 25 years of use, my knife is now finally being retired."

Diplomatic Traveler

Not all travelers encounter such hair-raising adventures. Sometimes the perils of traveling can amount to no more the annoyance of discovering that your luggage is coming apart, or that the plugs don't fit the sockets. The Australian Consul in Dublin, B. C. Hill told how his pocket knife made his life easier in many ways:

"I came across Victorinox knives in Switzerland when I was General Consul in Geneva in 1964. Since then my own personal knife, a Traveller, has been my constant companion. I find this pocket knife extremely practical since my work often requires me to fly from one end of the world to the other. When I arrive I frequently have to change the plugs on my personal electrical equipment, put up tie racks etc. My pocket knife always serves me extremely well. My knife has proven indispensable on my travels. It's impossible to carry a toolbox with you at all times when you're traveling by plane. Your knives offered the best alternative in those situations and have shown themselves to be useful in other ways for my son-in-law. Until quite recently he served as a career officer in the Australian Army; in this capacity he served in Vietnam for a year from 1965 to 1966. Before he returned to the Far East I sent him one of your knives, a Champion. He later told me that this knife had been indispensable to him during his

twelve-month active service, particularly on jungle patrols. In fact, the knife was so popular that he had to keep an eye out to make sure he did not lend it to his brothers-in-arms for longer than was necessary!"

The Army Knife at War

Many armed forces throughout the world order Victorinox knives for their soldiers' personal survival kits. Even personnel who are not issued with the knives officially, have been known to carry them in addition to the regulation survival kits. When US Air Force pilot Scott O'Grady was stranded in the Balkan woods for days he made considerable use of his Swiss Army Knife to help him survive the ordeal. Another dramatic story comes from an officer in the Argentine Navy whose life was saved by a Swiss Army Knife during the Falklands War:

"During an assault we came under fire from three snipers. I took one bullet through the right elbow, another on the side (pulverising three ribs), and one on the Victorinox Explorer pocket knife that was hanging in its pouch from my web belt, just in front of my left groin. The shot landed straight on one of the pocket knife's red plastic sides with a strength enough to embed the whole thing in my groin, but stopping short of the femoral artery.

"That night, as I woke from my second session of surgery, one of my comrades was standing by my bed, still in his combat camos. He casually presented me with the remains of the knife that had saved my life. The knife now stands on a plaque in the wardroom in Mar del Plata Naval Base."

The Great Survivor

Despite their intricate design, these knives are built to last. They have survived many accidents and seem to be able to withstand the roughest treatment. A cyclist from Canada recounted that his knife was used to repair a broken chain during a mountain cycling race. Using the knife's awl and a large piece of granite as a hammer, he removed the defective link in the chain so that it could be replaced, and was amazed to find that his knife still closed smoothly and survived to serve him another day. One of the most astonishing survival stories comes from Gilbert V. Levin in 1991.

"In 1973 I had installed my new invention for sewage treatment at Seneca Falls, New York. One morning as I was crossing the bridge over the aeration tank of the treatment plant, I saw that the setting of one of the instruments was incorrect. I immediately took out my reliable Swiss army knife to carry out the necessary adjustments. The knife slipped out of my hand and fell into the aeration tank. The function of the aeration tank in a treatment plant is to oxidize organic waste. This oxidizing environment is very corrosive to metals.

"Four years later I received a small parcel by mail with a note from the supervisor of the plant at Seneca Falls. The parcel contained my knife. In 1977 he had emptied the aeration tank. At the bottom of the tank they saw my Swiss Army knife. I looked at it and was astonished to see that it was in such good condition. The only defect of any note was that the spring for the scissors was missing, it had dissolved. It also

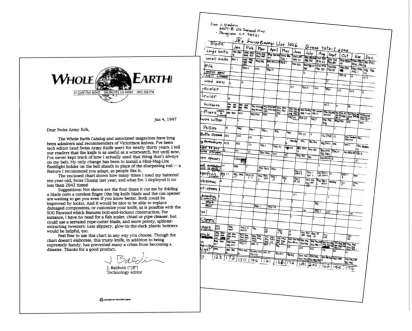

had a bit of rust on the aluminum parts for keeping the blades separate. The plastic casing and cover had only suffered very minor damage where the toothpick and the tweezers were inserted. I can assure you that very few products would have been able to survive treatment like this; all their components would have simply dissolved or simply 'disappeared.' "

Diving Knives

A marine biologist from Florida wrote to Victorinox in 1970 urging them to advertise their knives for the American market:

"During the entire month of August, I, and three of my colleagues, lived on the Ocean Floor in the Virgin Islands. During this prolonged saturation diving experiment of the US Government I used your knife daily, even taking it with me onto the coral reef. Although it received no care or maintenance it never was difficult to open and it showed no signs of rust or corrosion. Your knife is rapidly becoming THE knife for people, like marine scientists, who require a precision-made, reliable, maintenance-free, knife and tool set.'

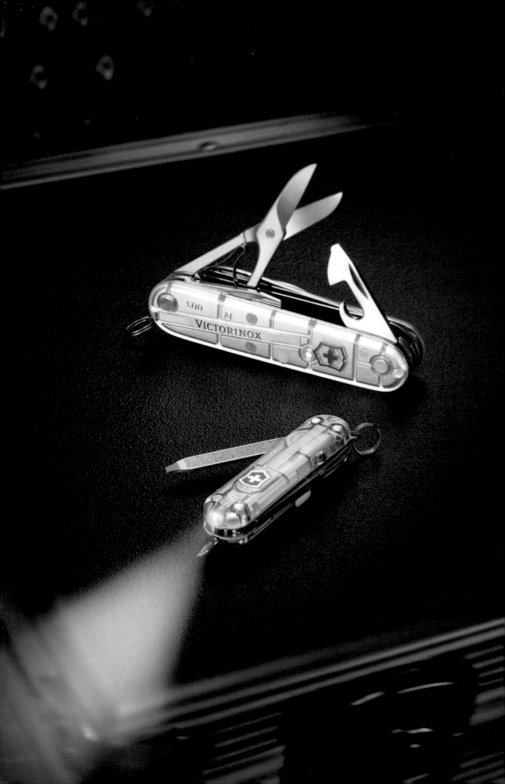

Index